BON

The L. Ron Hubbard Series

BRIDGE PUBLICATIONS, INC.
5600 E. Olympic Boulevard
Commerce, California 90022

ISBN 978-1-4031-9894-5

Cover artwork & illustrations: pp. iv, 13, 15, 50, 67, 106 *Detective Fiction Weekly, Adventure, Argosy Magazine* is © 1935, 1936, 1937 Argosy Communications, Inc. All Rights Reserved. Reprinted with permission from Argosy Communications, Inc.; pp. 43, 122, 128 *Unknown* copyright © by Street & Smith Publications, Inc. Reprinted with permission of Penny Publications, LLC; *Thrilling Wonder, Thrilling Adventures, Thrilling Western*, pp. 8, 10, 50 © 1935, 1948, 1949 Standard Magazine, Inc. Reprinted with permission of Hachette Filipacchi Media; pp. iv, 50, 80 *Top-Notch Magazine, Western Story, Wild West Weekly, Romantic Range* © and ™ Condé Nast Publications and are used with their permission; pp. iv, 46, 52, 132, 154 Edd Cartier.

Special acknowledgment is made to the L. Ron Hubbard Library for permission to reproduce photographs from his personal collection. Additional credits: pp. 1, 7, 51, 61, 95, 119, 145, 165, back cover Pagina/Shutterstock.com; p. 2 courtesy of New York Public Library; p. 11 Frescomovie/Shutterstock.com; p. 19 Alexkar08/Shutterstock.com; pp. 30, 92/93 Hulton Collection/Getty Images; pp. 31, 34 Tatiana53/Shutterstock.com; pp. 34/35 Keellla/Shutterstock.com; pp. 42, 167 courtesy of Jay Kaye Kline; p. 44 courtesy of the Syracuse University Library; pp. 71, 84, 116/117 Time & Life Pictures/Getty Images; p. 74 courtesy of Mark Wanamaker; pp. 80, 157 R-studio/Shutterstock.com; p. 83 courtesy of the Library of Congress; p. 111 Steve Albano/Shutterstock.com; pp. 112/113 Corbis; p. 115 David Hughes/Shutterstock.com; p. 136 courtesy of College Archives, Special Collections, Middlebury College, Vermont; p. 156 courtesy of University of California, Santa Cruz.

John W. Campbell, Jr., letters of January 23, 1939, March 21, 1939 and April 19, 1939 appearing on pages 41–47 courtesy of AC Projects, Inc.

Robert A. Heinlein letters of March 26, 1949, December 15, 1980 and December 16, 1982 appearing on pages 157, 167, 169 courtesy of University of California, Santa Cruz.

Printed in the United States of America

The L. Ron Hubbard Series: Literary Correspondence—English

RON

The L. Ron Hubbard Series

LITERARY CORRESPONDENCE
LETTERS & JOURNALS

Bridge

PUBLICATIONS, INC. ®

CONTENTS

An Introductory Note

From the greater treasury of L. Ron Hubbard Archives comes a highly illuminating collection of personal letters and autobiographical journals. All told, these materials span the whole of L. Ron Hubbard's life—from his first extraordinary steps of adventure and discovery to his ultimate triumph with the founding of Dianetics and Scientology. Accordingly (and albeit representing but a fraction of his archival material), these papers provide exquisite depth and color to a most extraordinary life. Hence, this special, supplemental edition within the larger L. Ron Hubbard Series: L. Ron Hubbard's Letters & Journals.

The Literary Correspondence of
L. Ron Hubbard

PRESENTED IN THIS PUBLICATION IS A SIGNIFICANT selection of correspondence from the literary life of L. Ron Hubbard. Although a full appreciation of that life is only possible from a reading of the companion to this publication, *L. Ron Hubbard Series: Writer—The Shaping of Popular Fiction,* let us at least consider the broader strokes.

Long synonymous with high adventure and far-flung exploration, the name L. Ron Hubbard originally graced the pages of some two hundred rough-stock periodicals, otherwise known as the pulps and likewise synonymous with raw adventure in exotic locales. Included among his more than fifteen million words of pre-1950 fiction were tales spanning all primary genres: action, intrigue, mysteries, westerns, even the occasional romance. Enlisted to "humanize" a machine-dominated science fiction, the name L. Ron Hubbard next became synonymous with such utterly classic titles as *Final Blackout* and *To the Stars*—rightfully described as among the most defining works in the whole of the genre. No less memorable were his fantasies of the era, including the perennially applauded *Fear,* described as a pillar of all modern horror. Indeed, as the critics tell us, there is finally no speculative writer of note—from Ray Bradbury to Stephen King—who does not owe a literary debt to the early tales of L. Ron Hubbard.

With the founding of Dianetics and Scientology (the fruition of research actually financed through those fifteen million words of fiction), Ron withdrew from the literary arena for some thirty years.... Whereupon he returned to the field in the early 1980s with two monumental blockbusters: the internationally bestselling *Battlefield Earth* and the ten-volume *Mission Earth* (each volume likewise topping international bestseller lists in what amounted to an unprecedented publishing event). Thereafter, and with worldwide sales of LRH novels well into the millions, we come to the real appeal of this publication: the letters of an author who now stands among the most influential, enduring and widely read writers of the twentieth century.

The aspiring author, 1929

In one way or another, the letters here illuminate all we have so briefly sketched. From a hopeful winter of 1934 comes a precious hundred dollars courtesy of an Ed Bodin, literary agent to a host of desperate authors fighting for a place in that keenly competitive pulp fiction market. From a somewhat healthier summer of 1935 comes Ron's formal greeting to readers of *Adventure* as "a tall red-haired chap with a service background." From an altogether prosperous 1936 comes the editorial back-and-forth for a first full-length novel, while Florence McChesney of *Five-Novels Monthly* wonders "if you're doing a flying story for me next." Then follows a contemplative exchange of notes on characterization, an equally contemplative sequence from a thoughtful season in Manhattan and several wry words on fencing with irascible editors. While very much to the point of the troublesome editor comes a choice selection of letters to and from John W. Campbell, Jr., on the reshaping of speculative fiction despite John W. Campbell.

The greater point: For all we have seen in explanation of L. Ron Hubbard's literary triumph, here is the deepest view yet. Here is the huddling with editors to firmly lay down story lines, then the "wondering what the hell they'll find wrong this time, certain that it will be different than the last." Here is that "jittery frame of mind" at the first blank page and "all the fun I want in twisting plots and trying out stunts of technique." Here is the crafting of tales to satisfy the banker, plumber, bellhop and grocer—all while striving for perfection, "because if we achieve perfection then we have come as close to the activity of the Self as a mortal can get." In short, here is the literary life of an author as only an author can express it, and then only to another who lives it.

In addition to personal correspondence as such, we include Ron's 1936 open letter to New York columnist O. O. McIntyre in defense of the pulps and his equally open advice to "word-weary" fledglings. We further include his letters in farewell to the pulps from the late 1940s, his notes to Robert Heinlein upon returning to a literary life in the 1980s and much else relating to what followed from the very crucial "...and then, by God, I'll write." ■

Editors, Manuscripts and the BUSINESS OF WRITING

Editors, Manuscripts and the
Business of
Writing

"I WAS BORN IN NEBRASKA AND THREE WEEKS LATER WENT to Oklahoma," or so L. Ron Hubbard introduced himself to the no-nonsense readers of *Adventure*. To what he supplies in the way of his thumbnail sketch, let us add the following: His initial submissions had been furiously pounded out through a six-week stint following his return from a Puerto Rican mining expedition. He wrote blind—which is to say, without benefit of editorial direction—and submitted to the slush pile—which is to say, without benefit of known representation. Nevertheless, he managed to net himself half a dozen crucial sales by the end of 1933, whereupon he joined the stable of agent Ed Bodin and the "regular contributor" lists of such top-line publications as *Five-Novels Monthly* and *Argosy*.

Then, too, and given no issue would carry more than a single story from any one author, he had further launched the careers of Ken Martin and Lt. Jonathan Daly, i.e., the first of several LRH pen names and thus the point of Bodin's letter of late 1934. In particular: that Leo Margulies of Standard Magazines had apparently purchased an anonymous story so plainly smacking of L. Ron Hubbard he immediately suspected a plagiarizing hand. In fact, L. Ron Hubbard had indeed penned that story, but Bodin had removed the byline (presumably to place the tale in an issue already featuring LRH). In either case, here is the Bodin suggestion of a "Legionnaire Longworth," which, by turns, became "Legionnaire 148," and thus the later pen name of several LRH adventures with French colonial settings.

Also pursuant to this business of writing comes the classic back-and-forth on plots and money, with the likes of Florence McChesney of *Five-Novels Monthly* and a William Kostka of *Detective Fiction Weekly*. Additionally for consideration is Ron's missive to Jack Byrne from Hollywood, where he was inconveniently ensconced scripting a soon-to-be box office smash entitled *The Secret of Treasure Island* at Columbia Pictures.

Outside Port Orchard, Washington, where many an LRH tale was authored through the late 1930s

There is significantly more concerning Ron's first foray into hardback novels with *Buckskin Brigades* and on those imaginative realms ruled by *Astounding Science Fiction* editor John W. Campbell, Jr. But our immediate point is merely this: although popularly described as an aristocrat of high adventure or a leading light of science fiction, L. Ron Hubbard actually wrote them all—two-fisted westerns, white-knuckled thrillers, brooding mysteries and even the occasional heart-throbber for Miss Fanny Ellsworth's *Ranch Romances*. ∎

ASSOCIATE EDITOR
THE WRITER'S REVIEW
CINCINNATI, OHIO

NATIONAL SECRETARY 1934
AMERICAN FICTION GUILD

EDITOR "THE MANUSCRIPT MAN" COLUMN
BIRMINGHAM NEWS-AGE-HERALD
BIRMINGHAM, ALA.

MARKET-TIP COLUMNIST
CALIFORNIA ART NEWS

FORMER NEWSPAPER COLUMNS:
LETTERS TO LUCIFER
WEEKLY NUMBERSCOPE
ED BODIN'S EDITORIAL

ED BODIN
AUTHOR'S EXECUTIVE
151 FIFTH AVENUE
NEW YORK CITY

11 YEARS WITH PUBLISHERS OF
COLLIER'S
AMERICAN MAGAZINE
WOMAN'S HOME COMPANION
COUNTRY HOME

TELEPHONES:
ALgonquin 4-3310
ALgonquin 4-6171

December 26, 1934

Dear Hubbard:

Here's the deep dark secret which you will have to keep mum on your life. In other words, don't dare tell Leo or anyone that you are the author of that story you sent me.

I took it up to Leo and told him here was a writer who had to keep his name secret for alimony reasons and that I could deliver him more material from the same pen.

This morning he called me up and wanted to know if it was a plagiarism for it was a damn good yarn, but the best he could offer was $100. I told him to send the check. Then he wanted to know who the author was and if he had ever heard of him. All I said, I would guarantee on my own rep that it wasn't a plagiarism and that I was pledged to secrecy on the name and couldn't tell my own mother.

Suppose you give me some pen name to keep in my files as I don't want to keep the docket on you in your own name in case one of my assistants should spill the beans, someday accidently. This would sour Leo toward me too.

Frankly, I'd like to get you into LIBERTY on some adventure stuff. I've sold LIBERTY over 50,000 words of adventure within the last few weeks. How about a name like Legionnaire Longworth, or some name we could build?

But of course, that's up to you. Just keep it mum that I have any of your stuff and someday the story of your secret trail will make good reading.

Respectfully,
Ed Bodin

Thrilling Adventures
Thrilling Detective
Thrilling Love
Thrilling Ranch Stories
Thrilling Western
Sky Fighters
The Lone Eagle
The Phantom Detective
Popular Western
Popular Detective

STANDARD MAGAZINES, Inc.
22 WEST 48th STREET
NEW YORK

Cable Address
"MAGSTAND"

February 26, 1935

Mr. L. Ron Hubbard
222 Riverside Drive
New York City

Dear Ron:

There's a gaping hole in the inventory of THRILLING ADVENTURES—that just must be filled.

The requirements are simple—a fast moving action story, locale, any spot on earth. Nothing barred—from westerns, pseudo-scientific, detective, costume to the good old-fashioned he-man American soldier of fortune running amuck around the world.

And all lengths—from two thousand word short-shorts to twenty thousand word novelettes. And we have no taboos because of an odd length.

We'll pay one cent a word—with a quick decision and prompt payment on acceptance. Have you anything on hand to shoot along?

Sincerely yours,
LEO MARGULIES
Editorial Director

Left L. Ron Hubbard headlining *Thrilling Adventures,* then under editorial stewardship of the ever-dapper Leo Margulies

Editors, Manuscripts and the Business of Writing   11

POPULAR PUBLICATIONS, Inc.
205 East 42nd Street, New York, N. Y.

July 24, 1935

L. Ron Hubbard, Esq.
Cannondale
Conn.

Dear Hubbard:

In looking over your autobiographical notes, I wish you had been more explicit about the Marine experience and other experiences.

All you fellows get a little self-conscious when you write about yourselves, and I wish you would do this over in a more definite and serious vein and mail it tomorrow, so that I will have it Friday to send to the printers.

Much obliged—and good luck.

Sincerely,
Howard Bloomfield
Editor

THE CAMP-FIRE

where readers, writers, and adventurers meet

by L. RON HUBBARD

*L. RON HUBBARD joins our Writers' Brigade
with his Leatherneck yarn, "He Walked to War." Hubbard is
a tall red-haired chap with a service background, his father being
an officer. He introduces himself at the Camp-Fire:*

I WAS BORN IN NEBRASKA and three weeks later went to Oklahoma. From there to Missouri, then to Montana. When I was a year old, they say I showed some signs of settling down, but I think this is merely rumor. Changing locales from the Pacific Coast to the Atlantic Coast every few months, it was not until I was almost twelve that I first left the United States. And it was not until I was sixteen that I headed for the China Coast.

In spite of changing schools, I received an education. I have some very poor grade sheets which show that I studied to be a civil engineer in college.

Civil engineering seemed very handsome at the time. I met the lads in their Stetsons from Crabtown to Timbuktu and they seemed to lead a very colorful existence squinting into their transits. However, too late, I was sent up to Maine by the Geological Survey to find the lost Canadian border. Much bitten by seven kinds of insects, gummed by the muck of swamps, fed on johnny cake and tarheel, I saw instantly that a civil engineer had to stay far too long in far too few places and so I rapidly forgot my calculus and slipstick and began to plot ways and means to avoid the continuance of my education. I decided on an expedition into the Caribbean.

It was a crazy idea at best and I knew it, but I went ahead anyway, chartered a four-masted schooner and embarked with some fifty luckless souls who haven't ceased their cursings yet. Our present generation just doesn't take to salt horse, dried peas, and a couple quarts of water a day.

But the expedition did the trick. I did not have to return to college. Instead I returned to the West Indies.

I might remark upon a coincidence which has always amazed me. While in the West Indies I discovered signs of gold on an island and, harboring the thought that the *Conquistadores* might have left some gold behind, I determined to find it.

China, 1928

China, 1928

Tumon Beach, Guam, 1927

Doris Hamlin, schooner aboard
which he sailed the Caribbean, 1932

After half a year or more of intensive search, after wearing my palms thin wielding a sample pick, after assaying a few hundred sacks of ore, I came back, a failure.

But a month after my return to Maryland, I discovered a vein of honey-comb quartz in the back pasture. The body of ore was tremendous, the visible vein several yards wide at the narrowest. Under the $20.67 an ounce, it assayed $82.34 a ton, and it is now worth about $145 a ton. However, to mine it takes money and I would have to stay close to Maryland. It's still there.

Chronological narration, in this short sketch, is impossible. Therefore, permit me to jump about a bit.

I was once convinced that the future of aviation lies in motorless flight. Accordingly I started gliding and soaring with the rest of the buzzards, and finally succeeded in establishing a record which has no official existence whatever and no reason, indeed, for existing. I traveled better than eighty miles an hour for twelve minutes in a soaring plane, maintaining the same altitude about an airport which is set on a flat plain. Answer: Heat lift from the circling concrete road.

From there I went into power flight, the high spot of which came on a barnstorming trip through the Mid-West in a five-lunged crate which staggered rather than flew. All one summer, I tried very hard to meet St. Pete, but evidently that gentleman either lost my name from the roll or my luck is far better than I think it is.

Unfortunately, in my Asiatic wanderings, no one, not even Hindu fortune tellers, thought to inform me that I would someday make my living with a typewriter and so I completely forgot to conduct myself informatively and devoted my time to enjoying life.

In Peiping, for instance, I did not avail myself of photographic impressions I might well have gained. I completely missed the atmosphere of the city, devoting most of my time to a British major who happened to be head of the Intelligence out there.

In Shanghai, I am ashamed to admit that I did not tour the city or surrounding country as I should have. I know more about 181 Bubbling Well Road and its wheels than I do about the history of the town.

In Hong Kong...well, why take up space?

Time after time, people accuse me of having been in the Marines. Pushed right up against the wall, I am forced to admit a connection with that very cosmopolitan outfit, however short lived and vague. I was once a top-kicker in the 20th because, as they sing in Shin-ho,

> I walked down the street
> Without a cent in my jeans,
> And that is the reason
> I joined the Marines.

I am not sure that calling squads east and west fits a man for writing, but it does give him a vocabulary.

One thing I might mention in connection with the leathernecks, most of the fiction written about them is of an intensely dramatic type, all do and die and *Semper Fidelis* and the dear old flag.

Left LRH photographs from the landscapes of his youth and vistas of his tales

To me the Marine Corps is a more go-to-hell outfit than the much lauded French Foreign Legion ever could be. The two are comparable in many ways. God knows what you'll find in either, from college professors to bellhops. Just why the disappointed lover has to sneak off for North Africa all the time is a riddle. More men have taken refuge in the Corps than in the Legion and, judging from association, leathernecks certainly lead a sufficiently exciting existence.

I've known the Corps from Quantico to Peiping, from the South Pacific to the West Indies, and I've never seen any flag waving. The most refreshing part of the U.S.M.C. is that they get their orders and start out and do the job and that's that. Whether that job was to storm the heights of Chapultepec so that the United States Army could proceed, or to dislodge a crazy gentleman named John Brown from an arsenal at Harpers Ferry, or to knock off a few Boxers for the glory of England, your marine went and did the job and then retired to bind up his wounds while everyone else went on parade.

Let it suffice. This is more than a thumbnail sketch, but I hope it's a passport to your interest. I know a lot of you out there, and I haven't heard from you in years. I know I haven't had any address, but I'm certain the editor will forward my mail.

When I get back from Central America, where I'm going soon, I'll have another yarn to tell.

DELL PUBLISHING COMPANY, INC.
149 MADISON AVENUE
NEW YORK

GEORGE T. DELACORTE, JR.
PRESIDENT

CABLE ADDRESS "DELLPUB"

360 N. MICHIGAN AVE.
CHICAGO, ILL.

October 16, 1936

Dear Ron:

Okay for "The Renegades." It's wild, but not too wild. The main thing is that the story has "it"—appeal to readers, without insulting their intelligence. Next on the book is the popular yarn of the air. I haven't had any readers' comment on "Sky Birds Dare!" but if the readers don't like that, I disown them—it was a darn good story.

I see that a British publisher is anxious to back a flight rivaling the American publishers' Around-the-World affair, which has been getting large publicity. And I wonder if you couldn't write a whale of a good air yarn about international rivals on a flight like that. Keep the American-British or whatever angle clean straight sportsmanship, so far as the backers are concerned, but drag in a lot of dirty work by unscrupulous guys on one side or the other—preferably both. However, don't let the suggestion cramp your style. Write what you please. Air is the idea...and you do it darn well. Whatever you do, keep the next story in mind—the Alaskan yarn, which I'm counting on. I rather thought you could use flying in it, but if you're doing a flying story for me next, maybe the flying in the Alaskan yarn had better be incidental. And so—anyway, let me know what you propose to do.

By the way, both Reynolds and Scruggs are entering the Little-Brown novelette contest, not with too optimistic an eye on the prizes, but with hopes of being bought for publication anyway. Are you competing? I think the length runs between about 15,000 and 35,000—short novel length.

Adios for now.

With all good wishes,
Florence

Sky Birds Dare! 1936

DELL PUBLISHING COMPANY, INC.
149 MADISON AVENUE
NEW YORK
CABLE ADDRESS "DELLPUB"

GEORGE T. DELACORTE, JR.
PRESIDENT

360 N. MICHIGAN AVE.
CHICAGO, ILL.

November 1936

Dear Ron:

The Legion story is oke and the check will go through next week. I expected a story of China, but it makes no never mind. And the Legion story will run in the December issue, along with a story of China which came in a few weeks ago.

The last issue, November's, drove me quite mad, as everything ran too long and I had to break my fool neck cutting the magazine to bits. What fun! And did I cuss out the authors, the printer and the editor—mostly the editor, too—when I ran into that jam! You see why I have fits when your stories run too long? I even cut in editing, and they still come out too long and put me in a hole. So ——

What do you want to do next, and when do you think you can do it? Or has Hollywood got you in its maw? She's a fickle jade, so don't expect too many favors from her. And don't let your magazine markets drop, if you can help it.

I've been running around town like somebody with the devil on his heels, and all for no good reason. And I found a marvelous restaurant called Boni's, which is like no other Italian place in town—the food is so good that it ought to be called by some more celestial name, and the service is likewise.

My sister and her husband arrive Saturday night. I haven't seen her in seven years, and Dad hasn't seen her in eleven. Much excitement for the McChesneys. Hope I live through it!

Greetings to everybody—
Florence

1212 Gregory Way
Bremerton, Wash.
February 1, 1937

Florence McChesney
Editor, FIVE NOVELS
149 Madison Ave.
New York City

Dear Florence;

Herewith enclosed is VANGUARD TO STEEL. As you are the prize titleer, I have let the working title stick.

Ahead of me I have a long line of syllables but now that I've turned this one out for you I can attack them in a little better frame of mind. For two reasons: I didn't wholly let you down and there's always the chance of a check for it. These reasons are both very powerful.

Writing long stuff is all right, especially when you have received an advance. But when there is a tie-up on a novel, the poor writer, who has done nothing but work on it suddenly discovers that he has neglected his regular markets and is momentarily in a financial slump. This seems to be the danger of novels. No wonder the boys treat them with fear and trembling and also with curled lips. Leave it to the Hollywood lawyers to put a red flag in front of the check line by way of contract clauses.

I hear tell you're having a most warm winter. Out here, of all things, it has snowed steadily for weeks—unheard of in this country. I wonder if Roosevelt didn't shift the climate around too.

I thought I was coming to New York and then I thought I was coming and now I don't know what to think. So I don't think any more than I have to. I work and hope for the best.

This only seems to prove that no matter how far afield I may stray, I'll probably always be going around muttering to myself, "Gee, I think it's about time I did one for Florence." You don't know how comfortable it is to look back at the record book and know that the backbone of my career is FIVE NOVELS. Through long experience I can usually read the ms, think it over and then predict success or failure. Such steadiness of decision and such even choice is a feather in your cap. For most editors I write in a very jittery frame of mind, wondering what the hell they'll find wrong this time, certain that it will be different than the last. Which is probably the reason your lads work so faithfully and steadily for you.

Although rates do make a difference, most of your writers will keep on with the editor who is the most consistent in reports because that way lies a comfortable peace of mind.

For instance your one remark has been, on actual style, that sometimes I would get confused in who was doing what. I pay particular attention to that now. Your comment on plot was that my yarns are sometimes wild. I have been slowly cutting down the improbability and I want to know when I reach a normal level. Outside of this, there isn't anything to keep me up in the air about what to do next.

I do not mean to intimate that I am smugly satisfied as to an assured acceptance. Far from that. But I know you won't throw one back at me unless you have very definite reasons—the fact which marks the good editor. No flattery that, because it is backed by the way Bruner and Scruggs and Holmes and Reynolds and I stick to our twenty thousand worders for FIVE NOVELS.

Vanguard to Steel, published as *All Frontiers Are Jealous,* June 1937

I know of no other magazine which is able to keep a consistent array of material.

If you want to know how you have improved my style and smoothed my work, compare, for instance, THE BRAVE DARE ALL and SEA FANGS. And there's plenty of room between the former and some future story.

Ah, well, wish I could drop in and cuss and discuss things with you.

Best regards,
Ron

Rt. 1—Box 452
Port Orchard, Wash.
April 22, 1937

Mr. William Kostka
Editor, DETECTIVE FICTION WEEKLY
280 Broadway
New York City

Dear Mr. Kostka;

Enclosed, find FANGS OF THE TIGER,[*] 10,500 word novelette which I tailored for D.F.W. on the pattern of the stories I used to write for your excellent book.

Due to the press of other affairs, I have not submitted a story to D.F.W. for over six months, but as I expect to have a clear slate ahead, even while south this spring, this lack of good sense on my part will be compensated to the best of my ability.

Unfortunately I have been stuck on this Coast for eight months, doing long stuff, and I have gotten entirely out of contact with my markets except through the able hands of Mr. Ed Bodin, my agent, who should receive the report on this story. If there is any particular type of story you wish and if there is anything in my repertoire you would like, I would be very flattered to hear from you.

So abysmal has my ignorance been that I had to phone Frank Pierce this morning to confirm the welcome news that you were the editor, and that I overlooked such a pleasant fact is demonstrative of the depth of my hermit's retreat. I mention this only in order that I may extend my belated best wishes and to apologize for not sending them sooner.

Hoping that you will find this latest effort of mine worthy of both your interest and your book and hoping also that it is at least good enough to invite further contacts on stories, I am

Sincerely,
L. Ron Hubbard

---

[*] *Owing to William Kostka's foreshortened stay at Detective Fiction Weekly (actually under four weeks), he was not to publish Fangs of the Tiger. The hard-boiled pages of Detective Yarns, however, was soon to see a similarly intriguing LRH mystery, Killer Ape.*

Right Killer Ape, June 1938

A DOZEN STORIES FOR A DIME

DETECTIVE YARNS

12 STORIES 10¢

ALL STORIES NEW!
NO REPRINTS!

JUNE

WHILE
CHINATOWN
SLEPT

a Harlan Dyce
novel, by

ARTHUR J. BURKS

also
L. Ron
Hubbard

Cyril
Plunkett

Norvell
W. Page

Hollywood, Calif.
July 1, 1937

Mr. John F. Byrne
Editorial Director,
MUNSEY PUBLISHING COMPANY
280 Broadway
New York City

Dear Mr. Byrne;

I thought that by this time I would be out of this hole. But no, I have to wait for a reading of something which has been finished for almost three weeks!

Don't you ever dare adopt Hollywood editorial methods!

The more I sit and stew the more stories I think up. I'm rolling a 20,000 for FN [FIVE-NOVELS MONTHLY] this week and then Saturday I think I'll have worked out a detective story for DFW and early next week I should have one for ARGOSY. A novelette with strong suspense, action, color, CAMERA!

Now why, says you, is L. Ron bursting out like this? The answer is obvious. I have been writing you stories which were greatly toned down because you once told me you did not like HURRICANE in FN. Very well. In this letter about STI* [SECRET OF TREASURE

ISLAND] you said you like the vigor of my style. Now in my poor, mild way I didn't click. You hated the impossible action of the FN story, not the color of the writing.

And I am afraid I have been handing you stories which were very, very pale. Now if I keep the same plot tempo I am now giving you and add to it the blaze and fire of my more usual work, I think we'll have something.

With nothing to do but think, I have been testing stories on people I know around here, trying to get straight about some things. Don't be alarmed. I do this every once in a while. The least intelligent of these selected guinea pigs chose my FN stories in preference to my ARGOSY yarns. This shocked me greatly. It was utterly impossible!

---

* Title of Ron's multipart matinee for Adventure Serials. It proved the biggest-grossing serial of the era and established L. Ron Hubbard as a screenwriter/script doctor par excellence.

And then, delving deeply I discovered they knew not what they said. They liked the zip and fire of my running description in FN but they did not like my plots for that book.

Well, you told me that first but I didn't get you straight. And now I think I have. You want vigorous but convincing, well-plotted yarns. You want colorful characters and settings.

Funny how long it takes a fellow to get these things soaked into his thick skull.

Now how about it? I value your opinion above any other editor's. If you'll let me give you all the flash and glory I can in my stories on the condition that I keep them calm as to plot, I can guarantee the popularity of everything you buy.

At one time you mentioned big scenes to me. Build up, you said, to a terrific wallop instead of giving us rapid wallops all packed close together.

And as constant study of technique is a hobby with me, I puzzled over ways and means to do this effectively and found a way which I tested on a western for ALL WESTERN. As it just sold and will be their lead it would seem to indicate that there was something to this method of handling your idea. I wish I could show you that story to illustrate what I mean.

In novelettes, I broke the story into chapters and placed each chapter in a new and interesting setting. (This is also one of your ideas. Remember what you said about variety of scenery in stories?) I stopped each chapter on a minor climax high, cut down in the beginning of the next to calmness and worked carefully but powerfully toward a higher climax which was, in turn, cut sharply off. That's sort of like music composition.

But this is in direct variance to what you told me about a central character. You said it should all be seen through his eyes.

Now, as a special dispensation for working so very hard for you, would it be possible for you to allow me to tell my story very objectively? I mean, let it revolve around one character, true enough. But as long as everything that happens concerns that character, could I, for instance, start a chapter with the villain and a dame and build up to the entrance of the hero a few pages later in the same chapter. This I assure you, is a trick which I have worked hard to perfect and as one 15,000 worder sold so fast that the edges of the check were burnt because I used this, I have gained some confidence in it as a rather individual pattern possessing the shocking power of a new 4,700-ft/sec. .22 bullet.

If I could do this new version of STI like that, I could guarantee you a story "worthy of both L. Ron Hubbard and ARGOSY" as you so kindly said once upon a time.

I am writing you all this because you have been of great help to me in the past and I very selfishly wish to avail myself of your reactions, wholly disregarding the fact that you are probably swamped with the regular run of the mill business.

Another thing I want to do in ARGOSY—if you'll let me. You stress *variety*. You might have noticed that I am intensely wary of becoming any kind of a story specialist. As you know I have sold the gamut of types: air-war, air, western, detective, love, terror, and even light love. That was for my own sanity. I get bored very swiftly if I hammer too long on one subject. The mainstay is, of course, adventure stories. But I think I have sold almost every kind of adventure story except the pseudo-scientific. And I want to do a bang-up job on one and sell it to you just because I have unique ideas of how one should be done.

My one passion is to build a name for variety—which was why I was so keen about doing those dangerous professions.

I have a phobia about getting in a rut, I suppose. At least the best way I have of keeping my stories alive is by writing all kinds.

You are very patient if you have read this far. Enough of that.

Last Saturday I had a good time driving around with Dick Wormser. He exacted a faithful promise from me however that I was not to tell you what he was doing down here and so I won't breathe a word about it. As a matter of fact he's sitting pretty—if *any* writer in Hollywood ever sat that way, which I doubt.

Had lunch today with George Bruce out on the MGM lot. He's doing well by himself, looking good. His office would make you writhe with envy (it made me squirm anyhow). All in blue leather. I sicced International Business Machines on him and they talked him into junking his famous Remingtons and sold him a new IBM electric writing machine like mine. I am still waiting for my commission which I intend to donate to the Home for Broken-Down Manual Mills.

I solemnly assured both Wormser and Bruce that they were now so high up in the world they wouldn't ever turn to the mags again and they agreed. And then very slyly with a cunning gleam in my eye, I said, "I sure am glad. That means I can sure roll it into ARGOSY with you boys out of the running."

Señor Byrne, if you have ever seen men deflate, grimace, writhe and take on the complexions of corpses, you'll know how Wormser and Bruce looked. I mean sad but murderous.

Of course they recovered and tried to pretend they cared not a jot. Oh yeah?

The mental attitude of a writer in Hollywood after the first week would be amusing if it were not so horribly pathetic. He has never seen so much money all in one pile before and he don't dare let go of the chance to get it.

But he has never seen such a dumb, wasteful, arrogant, hopeless jumble in his orderly magazine career and he is aghast. He realizes he is passing up those sweet days when he worked when he felt like it. He is missing the friendly camaraderie of his editors and fellow craftsmen. He is suddenly under a yellow banner emblazoned with a cross-barred S and the whole topic of every conversation into which he is projected is, "I make $xx,xxx a week."

The lost feeling gradually wears off as his viewpoint changes. Missing a chance to express himself in print he begins to use the most childish and vile language imaginable. His hero is always a "bastard" and his heroine is a "bitch" and if something is not up to the mark, he says it's so much _____. (Uncle Sam would get me on that one.)

In spite of some small success here, I am turning down all contracts and pulling my freight. I like to write for men like you and books like you print and I guess I'm somewhat unbalanced in that direction. I like my freedom. I fight hard for independent individualism. I love to tie into a yarn and try to make it blaze in print.

The mags will never lose me to the movies. NEVER, at any salary!

Given the impetus of getting out of this town, having had time to study my style a bit, I am now anxious to do only one thing: Write you novels better than any ever published in ARGOSY before. That is not anything but an ambition I am cherishing. With your help we'll perhaps be able to at least try for a worthy goal.

Hoping to see you this Fall and

Best regards,
L. Ron Hubbard

Route One—Box 452
Port Orchard, Wash.
Dec. 7, 1937

Miss Fanny Ellsworth
Editor, RANCH ROMANCES
515 Madison Ave.
New York City

Dear Miss Ellsworth;

I send you ROBIN HOOD OF THE RANGE.* I would like very much to have your reaction to this story so that I can angle others more closely.

In the past, Ed Bodin sent a few strays your way but I have no way of knowing your comment on them and Bodin is no longer handling my stories.**

Best regards,
L. Ron Hubbard

---

* *Eventually retitled* Boss of the Lazy B, *and appearing in the 10 September 1938 issue of* Western Story Magazine.

** *In the autumn of 1937, under wholly amicable circumstances, LRH left the Bodin stable to represent himself. Although he would never advertise the reasons for his departure, we know the agent had long lacked the wherewithal to routinely market subsidiary rights in Hollywood and abroad.*

Right View from Ron's Port Orchard, Washington, "Writer's Cabin"

On "Buckskin Brigades"

Inspired by Ron's youthful encounters with the Blackfeet of Montana, Buckskin Brigades would finally prove the most celebrated of all L. Ron Hubbard westerns. Described as a "vigorously authentic" tale "told through the mind and body of an American Indian," the story ultimately chronicles the tragic encounter between a then mighty Blackfoot Nation and an avaricious Hudson's Bay Company. Eventually published as a full-length novel from The Macaulay Company, Buckskin Brigades would enjoy an extraordinarily long shelf life, with extended critical acclaim for more than fifty years. While the work still lay in progress, however, Ron had toyed with the possibilities of serialization in Jack Byrne's Argosy. That Byrne eventually declined is, of course, incidental to Ron's thoughts on the matter and Byrne's oh-so-typical editorial input. ■

THE FRANK A. MUNSEY COMPANY

280 BROADWAY

New York

Argosy
Detective Fiction

Members
ALL FICTION FIELD

All-Story
Railroad Stories

November 27, 1936

Mr. L. Ron Hubbard
1212 Gregory Way
Bremerton, Washington

My dear Hubbard:

I'm glad to hear that you are interested in the serial because I have a hunch that you are going to do us a good yarn on this one. "Buckskin Brigades" is a very good title, I think.

I agree with you about the regular western fiction which fills so many of our magazines. These yarns as a whole are pretty dull stuff, it seems to me. I like to think of our ARGOSY westerns now as historical yarns. I believe too that the majority of adult readers in the field are also chiefly interested in historical aspects. Wherefore we can kill two birds by giving them the real thing as far as background goes and still develop the colorful fiction story in the bargain.

Let me know how your work progresses when you get a chance. Our ARGOSY sales have been showing a little pickup as you know, but we fell into a slump during the election period after seeming to be on our way in September. I think we are building solidly though and that we will keep on showing progress as we go along.

Best of luck,
Jack Byrne
Editor
ARGOSY

1212 Gregory Way
Bremerton, Wash.
December 8, 1936

Mr. Jack Byrne
Editor, ARGOSY
280 Broadway
New York City

Dear Mr. Byrne;

Enclosed is the synopsis of BUCKSKIN BRIGADES.

Except for a few minor plot changes which are always bound to creep into the actual writing as you well know, this is the way she goes.

It is carefully planned for effect more than anything else, and I think it will make a racy yarn. As a glance will tell you, it is based upon characters, not plot alone.

I have pooled the most exciting events of the fur trade and these, in their turn, have of course influenced the time spacing.

Apparently the beginning is a little slow, but for the sake of brevity I have omitted the form and have simply stated the facts. Cutbacks and inter-plot will speed it up.

As you wished, this will probably run between sixty and seventy thousand words as there will be no lack of suspense and interest and the subject, in all fairness to it, demands much more.

Probably you will wonder a little at the ending I have jotted here. Without this ending the whole structure will lean in the trite direction taken by so many costume novels. It is impossible to see that in this short summary which follows and in spite of what most writers seem to think, clairvoyance isn't a part of an editorial job. And so, as it will come out in its proper length, my idea, condensed, is this: The Indian in his backwoods was much better off without any contact on the turbulent white frontier, beset as it was with the turbulence of the fur brigades.

I am not yet satisfied with my research as several inquiries I have made to well-known ethnologists and friends up on Indian lore have not yet been returned to me. However, this is all pertinent to weapons, costume, hunting methods and woodcraft—small points, but very vital to the life thread of such a work.

I am also enclosing an airmail envelope for the return as I hope to start on this not later than the coming Sunday at which time I will have assembled everything, rolled up my sleeves, bought a new ribbon, emitted a war-whoop preparatory to getting into the spirit of the thing.

Best regards,
L. Ron Hubbard

Snake River, Washington, not far from where Ron authored *Buckskin Brigades*

THE FRANK A. MUNSEY COMPANY

280 BROADWAY

New York

Argosy
Detective Fiction

Members
ALL FICTION FIELD

All-Story
Railroad Stories

December 11, 1936

Mr. L. Ron Hubbard
1212 Gregory Way
Bremerton, Wash.

Dear Hubbard:

I see a great deal of promise in the material you have outlined for "Buckskin Brigades." As you can understand, I am not particularly concerned right now with the plot motion of the story or the incidents thereof: I know that you can handle these and weld them together into a harmonious whole. I do, however, like your people and the general situation. My chief injunction now is this: remember that you are selling a fiction story against a historical background; don't let things that have actually happened obstruct the free use of your imagination and the dramatization of what might have been.

A secondary point to watch is to see that we get the individual emotional reaction of the other characters as well as that of the hero to a certain extent. For instance, White Fox should not trail Yellow Hair with unalloyed beneficence, it seems to me. He should dislike certain tendencies the youngster shows, be deeply resentful of the fact that Michael is so aroused by the white girl when Little Star is waiting for him. I think too that Little Star should be quite a character—a warrior woman rather than a girl who waits complacently to be taken when our hero returns from the wars.

I also sense (I may be wrong on this) that there is need for additional personal problems as far as Michael is concerned. This is merely off-hand suggestion, but it occurred to me that in one of his early contacts with the whites, the leader of the whites would sense the potential value of this young fellow to his faction. He would get Michael drunk and have him take part in the attack against another faction in which various whites would be killed. Thus Michael wakes up in the morning with scalps at his belt and with his new found friends telling him of the terrific battle he has put up. He has no memory of it and must perforce accept their story as the truth. This, of course, will mean that if Michael is captured by the rivals he will immediately be drawn and quartered; and that his reputation as a tough son-of-a-gun goes throughout the country. This would be a factor against him in the eyes of Evelyn Lee. It would also give him an additional problem to solve, etc.

I note too a sort of tendency to have him rescued from various jams and captures by talking his way out or through the intercedence of a third party. Why not let him instead make spectacular daring escapes that would be in keeping with his character as the fastest running, the swiftest and truest arrow, the lightest man among the Blackfeet? When Take-Gun-Twice captures him, for example, why can he not outdo the great Iroquois in various Indian tests of strength and skill so that Take-Gun-Twice would first have to kill Michael before he can again claim to be the strongest and bravest among all the red men as was his boast.

I am just shooting these arrows into the air as off-hand suggestions. The purpose of them being merely to stimulate your thinking along the lines they indicate. Otherwise, I think everything shapes up excellently and I'll be very interested to see how the story works out.

Why not let me look at the first installment or the first two installments, say, when you have finished it. I might have some ideas that I could send along to you at that time which would be of assistance.

Sincerely,
Jack Byrne
Editor
ARGOSY

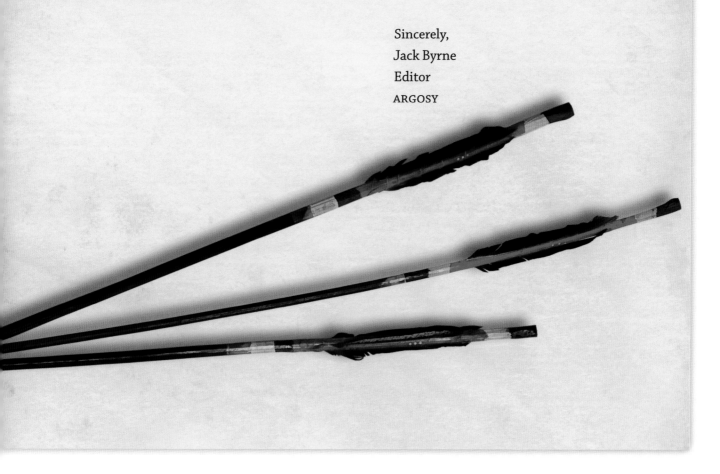

1212 Gregory Way
Bremerton, Wash.
January 18, 1937

Dear Mr. Byrne;

It was fine of you to speed up your reading on BUCKSKIN BRIGADES in view of the stacks of mss through which you daily have to swim and burn up a weekend as well.

Stage-fright is a recognized mental state, but syllable-scare ought to have its place in psychiatry. I guess I could have turned out that story hand over fist for any cheap market in the field, but when it came to placing it before you and ARGOSY I can tell you I didn't get much sleep while I was writing it. It was only after I really dug into the story for the story itself that I managed to partially shake off my jitters. In trying to make the grade I gave it a theme and an entirely different pattern and was altogether too intent upon pioneering a new type of frontier story to remember that, after all, it had to be *read* as well as written. And when I added palsy.......

Oh well, you haven't got time for excuses. All you want is results.

I have a story here now, ready to start, which will run sixty thousand and should take six weeks in the writing. Africa. Plenty of excitement in it and a couple unusual characters.

And please don't be too tough on me for BUCKSKIN BRIGADES because you know yourself that a writer is slam-bang up against his story and even though he is living it, thrilling to it, slaving on it, he very often fails to know whether the story is good or bad after he has finished it. I guess that was the case this time. When I was very young at this business I accepted my own reaction. But I've had too many I thought were bad accepted as good and too many good accepted as bad until I finally began to realize that, regardless of my capabilities, my knowledge of worth was too small for a second consideration. And now I carefully reserve my own judgment on anything and everything in spite of the effort put forth until someone who really knows about these things hands out sentence. An unhappy state of mind, I know, and one which, at first glance, might be considered servile. It is not.

And so, I don't think you'll find me guilty of any bitterness on any decision and as I am more interested in the truth than my feelings in the matter. After all, I only know my technique and have only had to develop craftsmanship. You were made responsible for the destiny of Munsey because you have proved over a long period that you are a past master at judging results as well as craftsmanship and technique, and as your position holds ten times the responsibility of a writer's and ten times the work, any writer who failed to recognize and abide by your authority would give himself the titles of ingrate and fool.

All of which may be off the subject, but I only wanted you to know that I am so far from repaying any judgment with condemnation that I appreciate a great deal your sacrifice of time. By the light of this novel I can see to type the next.

Best regards,
L. Ron Hubbard

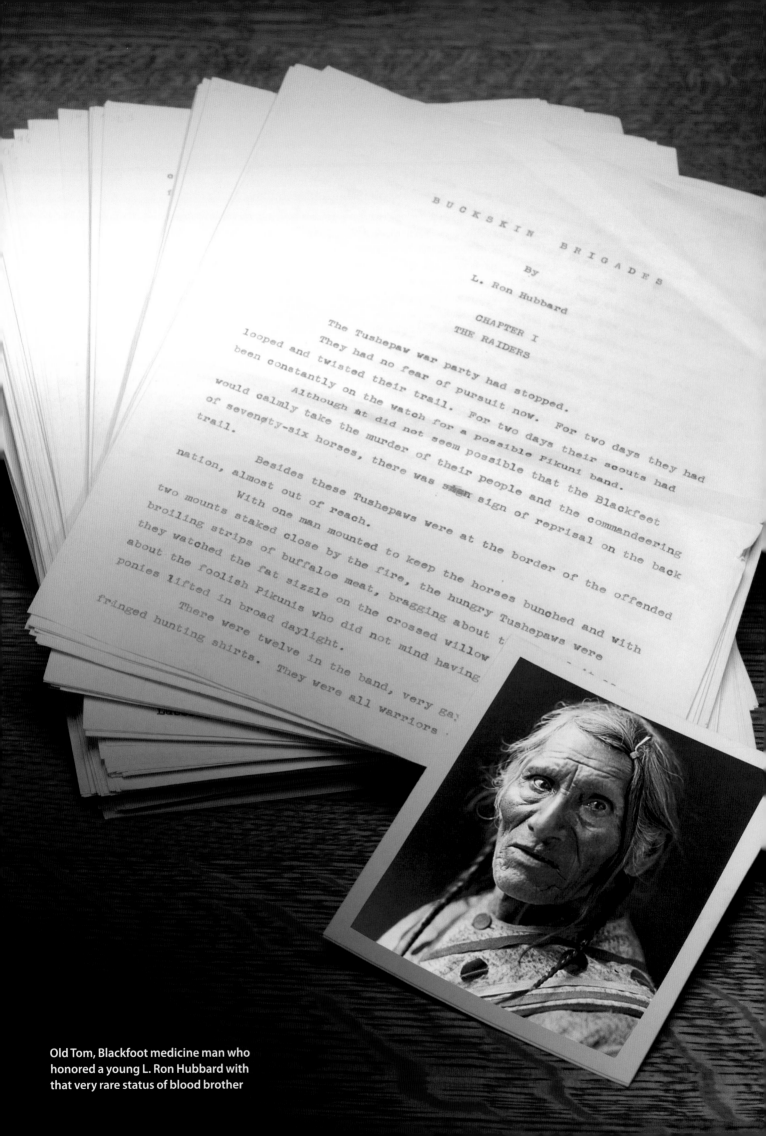

BUCKSKIN BRIGADES

By

L. Ron Hubbard

CHAPTER I

THE RAIDERS

The Tushepaw war party had stopped.

They had no fear of pursuit now. For two days they had looped and twisted their trail. For two days their scouts had been constantly on the watch for a possible Pikuni band.

Although it did not seem possible that the Blackfeet would calmly take the murder of their people and the commandeering of seventy-six horses, there was s--n sign of reprisal on the back trail.

Besides these Tushepaws were at the border of the offended nation, almost out of reach.

With one man mounted to keep the horses bunched and with two mounts staked close by the fire, the hungry Tushepaws were broiling strips of buffaloe meat, bragging about t-- - - -- they watched the fat sizzle on the crossed willow -- about the foolish Pikunis who did not mind having -- ponies lifted in broad daylight.

There were twelve in the band, very ga- - - - fringed hunting shirts. They were all warriors.

Old Tom, Blackfoot medicine man who
honored a young L. Ron Hubbard with
that very rare status of blood brother

THE MACAULAY COMPANY

381 FOURTH AVENUE • NEW YORK CITY

July 16th, 1937

Mr. L. Ron Hubbard
Route 1
Box 452
Port Orchard, Washington

Dear Mr. Hubbard:

BUCKSKIN BRIGADES will be published on July 30th. We have already sent six (6) copies to your agent, but I am sending on one copy directly to you by mail.

I presume you will let me see your new manuscripts as they are completed.

In regard to the Great Northern, I am in touch with these people, and as soon as I have some definite word as to what they will do, I will write to you again.

Sincerely yours,
Lee Furman
THE MACAULAY COMPANY

Buckskin Brigades, first edition,
The Macaulay Company, 1937

The John W. Campbell, Jr., Letters

No discussion of popular American literature through the 1930s is complete without mention of the frequently brilliant but infamously eccentric John W. Campbell, Jr. Readers of the L. Ron Hubbard Series: Writer—The Shaping of Popular Fiction will recall Mr. Campbell as that techno-minded editor of Astounding Science Fiction whom Ron first encountered when summoned to the offices of Street & Smith. Initially the relationship had been somewhat forced. Street & Smith had ordered Campbell to purchase all LRH submissions as a "humanizing" element to an otherwise inhuman genre and, understandably, Campbell turned bitter. In the end, however, the friendship proved as close as any Campbell would enjoy, as the undisputed and irascible czar of the science fiction realm. Also referenced in letters here is the LRH-Campbell collaboration on the shaping of modern fantasy as initially presented in the pages of Unknown and ultimately reflective in all one finds on modern fantasy shelves. ■

STORIES

79-89 SEVENTH AVENUE
NEW YORK, N. Y.

January 23, 1939

Mr. L. Ron Hubbard
Rt. 1, Box 452
Port Orchard, Wash.

Dear Ron:

I'm damn glad you'll be with us on the Arabian Nights stuff—and you needn't worry about having it yours. I've been telling a few of the boys to read Washington Irving as an example of pure fantasy and complete acceptance of magic, enchantment, et cetera, and adding that they aren't to do Arabian Nights because the field is preempted by you. It's been held open for you.

As soon as I can get hold of a few office copies of UNKNOWN, I'll send one on to you for perusal. "Sinister Barrier," "Trouble With Water" and "Where Angels Fear" are down the alley. "Death Sentence" and "Dark Vision" are pretty fair ideas. The other two are filling space for me acceptably. I'm having a hell of a time with it, because the genuinely first-rate fantasy I demand is hard to get: if it isn't genuinely first-rate, I'm not going to have the magazine I intend to, but just another fantasy magazine.

Basically, this is the philosophy I'm applying: All human beings like wishes to come true. In fairy stories and fantasy, wishes do come true. Adults with childish minds (average "adult" has the mind of a 14-year-old) don't dare to read "fairy stories," because their minds are afraid to acknowledge their interest in anything childish—they subconsciously realize their mental immaturity and, as a defense mechanism, avoid childish things.

Your true adult, with fully developed mind, can enjoy fantasy wholeheartedly if it's written in adult words and thought-forms, because, being absolutely confident of his own mental capacity, he doesn't have any sense of embarrassment if caught reading "childish stuff."

You get the same effect in the physical world where you find the big, powerful, capable man pretty generally peaceable, friendly, and willing to take ribbing easily because of an assured and unquestionable power. The little runt is apt to be belligerent, spiteful, and bitterly resentful if ribbed.

And every human being likes fantasy fundamentally. All we need is fantasy material expressed in truly adult forms. Every author who honestly and lovingly does that makes a name on it. Lord Dunsany, Washington Irving, Stephen Vincent Benét. In view of this, I have absolute confidence that this new magazine will inevitably become more or less of a fashion among truly adult people—and will be despised by the 14-year-old-minds.

I don't, personally, like westerns particularly, and, in consequence, haven't read your western stuff. But I'm convinced that you do like fantasy, enjoy it, and have a greater gift for fantasy than for almost any other type. The fact that editor after editor has urged you to do that type seems to me indication that you always have had that ability, and that, in avoiding it heretofore, you've suppressed a natural, and not common, talent. There are a lot of boys that turn out readable westerns, but only about three or four men in a generation that do top-notch fantasy.

And, as I say, I'm reserving the Arabian Nights to you entirely.

Regards,
JOHN W. CAMPBELL, JR.
Editor—UNKNOWN

February 1, 1939

Dear John;

    Received your letter and the first copy of UNKNOWN today, for both of which I thank you. I have not yet had a chance to read very deeply but it is very obvious that you have a magazine which ought to sell. The only thing which could possibly kill it would be the tendency common to most writers to try to make the reader *believe* by disbelieving the thing themselves in the form of the hero's stream of consciousness.

LRH

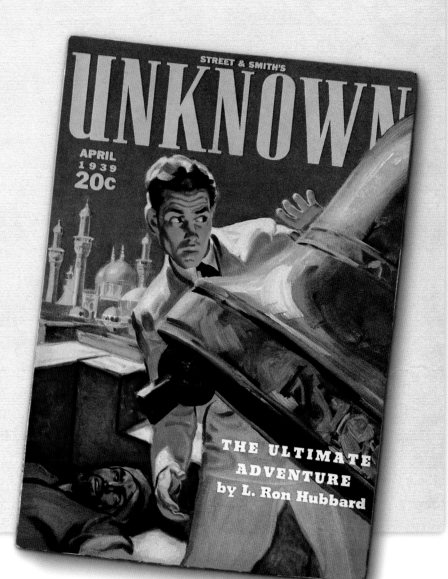

The April 1939 edition of *Unknown,*
bearing a first LRH tale of fantasy

STREET & SMITH PUBLICATIONS
INCORPORATED
SEVENTY-NINE SEVENTH AVENUE · NEW YORK, N. Y.

March 21, 1939

Mr. L. Ron Hubbard
Rt. 1, Box 452
Port Orchard, Wash.

Dear Mr. Hubbard:

The check—largest in UNKNOWN's brief history, and second largest in the combined UNKNOWN-ASTOUNDING history—is on its way. DON'T write more than 45,000 words after this, at least not in one chunk, please.

But, on the other hand, please start now on your next Arabian Nights yarn. What'll it be about? I'd like to get it in about four weeks. If not, then in six weeks. I'm having a hell of a time getting the long stuff, because I consistently and firmly bounce anything below grade B+, and all the novels seem to run about grade C+. And will you tell me when and if you're going to get over your mad at New York and move back where you're convenient? Considering the way the West Coast has treated you, I'd think you'd want to leave it.

You're going to have a sort of competition on Arabian stuff—but of a noncompetitive type, really. Silaki Ali Hassan, full-blooded Arab, is transcribing modern Arabic legends of the Yafri hill-country for us. They're different in tone from the Baghdad legends of the 1001 Nights.

And—just because UNKNOWN's going, don't forget ASTOUNDING still uses 85,000 words a month. If you must toss off a few shorts between chapters of the novels, how about your strongman from Alpha Centauri who sells the safety pins his father's factory makes?

Forgotten that guy? He sounded like nice material, as I remember it.

Sincerely,
JOHN W. CAMPBELL, JR.
Editor: UNKNOWN and
ASTOUNDING

Left The offices of Street & Smith, publisher of
Astounding Science Fiction and *Unknown*

THE GHOUL

EDD CARTIER

BY L. RON HUBBARD

I.

IRISH worked at the Burton Hotel in N'Yawk, though it wasn't quite as bad as that. Irish was strictly a N'Yawker, having established his right to that title very early in life by being born in Ireland—for it must be remarked that N'Yawkers are never born in N'Yawk.

Up to the time when he walks into our lives, his history had been very average, though very varied. As an orphan he

STREET & SMITH PUBLICATIONS
INCORPORATED
SEVENTY-NINE SEVENTH AVENUE · NEW YORK, N. Y.

JOHN W. CAMPBELL · *EDITOR* · *UNKNOWN*

April 19, 1939

Mr. L. Ron Hubbard
Rt. 1, Box 452
Port Orchard, Wash.

Dear Mr. Hubbard:

"Six Stolen Souls" becomes "The Ghoul" and we take it. However, I regret to state that I think it's about B, as against a straight A for your Arabian Nights stuff.

Irish feels forced—Stevie and your little ship-owner-Tiger guy were much more interesting. Also, humor stuff in the fantasy vein is too darned easy to come by; the horror angle is hard to get. This has no horror whatever. The ghoul isn't very menacing, really, because the story is, obviously, straight comedy, and comedy villains are always somewhat inefficient gentlemen.

I've got two long novels on the fire now, so, since you've gotten two successive covers (and something like $1600) I think maybe a novelette or two might be a pious idea. However, if you've got a long novel boiling in your mind, go ahead on that, and maybe for once I'll have a novel for the magazine a few days ahead of when I have to have it.

And may I point out that *my* telegram was much more stimulating to unknowing telegraph operators than yours? "Six stolen souls stolen or what? Not received. Need thirty to forty thousands. Reply."

You know—white slaving or something on a wholesale scale.

Regards,
JOHN W. CAMPBELL, JR.
Editor

Left L. Ron Hubbard's *The Ghoul* as originally published in the August 1939 issue of *Unknown*

CHAPTER TWO

In Defense of
THE PULPS

In Defense of
the Pulps

ALTHOUGH NOW ACKNOWLEDGED AS A FULLY VIBRANT force in popular American literature, the pulps were not infrequently maligned in their day. Charges included stock plots, dull renditions, extraneous violence and unabashed sensationalism—all of which was true, to a point. By the same token, however, those rough-cut and lurid-covered pulps also launched the likes of Dashiell Hammett, Raymond Chandler and many another who would finally prove just as integral to the shaping of American fiction as a Mark Twain or Ernest Hemingway. Then, too, and even more to the point of an L. Ron Hubbard, virtually all we know of modern speculative fiction arguably emerged from the pulps.

Nevertheless, the O. O. McIntyres had their day. A New York critic and political columnist (just to the right of Genghis Khan), McIntyre was typical of those who most condemned the pulps. He resented the sheer size of pulp readership—a full quarter of the American population, and very much including a lesser-educated working class. He resented that pervasive sense of heroic defiance woven through so many a grand pulp adventure, e.g., Ron's aforementioned "He Walked to War," telling of a footsore Marine fighting for the hell of it in a politically irrelevant banana republic. Then again, he almost certainly resented what the top-line pulp author earned; hence, the sly portrayal of the pulpateer as a glorified factory worker.

The LRH reply, actually intended as a letter to the editor, is as accurate as McIntyre is not. That Ron further felt obliged to add, "If you should happen to intimate to a pulpateer that his stories are trash, you are likely to be soundly punched in the nose," would seem to say everything else McIntyre need know about the hard-boiled crew from a great pulp kingdom. ∎

A few of the more than two hundred premier pulps featuring tales by L. Ron Hubbard

ead Payoff

RON HUBBARD
of "The Toughest Ranger," etc.

by
L. RON HUBBARD

Smoke Burnham, hurtling over jungle, caught by treacherous upsweeping winds of the mountains, knows he was racing against death. Seven planes had already gone aloft. Would his be the eighth?

A Dangerous Bet

of the AIR

PHANTOM PATROL

CHAPTER ONE

The

bidden Gold

by L. Ron Hubbard

With a dead man's hatred challenging him to the impossible, Kurt Reid stakes his life

Dead Man's Trick

The Headhunters
by
L. RON HUBBARD

Tom Christian, on a million-dollar trek into the jungle, is trapped by the headhunters and their renegade white leader

Travelers Headed for Trouble

BLACK
DANGER

by
RON
BBARD

El Opio went down, his arm shattered.

trying to prove his
finds Venezuela
spot for trouble

TOWERS

The Falcon Killer
By
L. Ron Hubbard

Both Stui Mai and Dmitri stared at Gaylord, wondering whether they should tell.

Brass
Keys to
Murder
by
Michael Keith

Sailors and longshoremen crowded into the room, their eyes eager with the prospect of a fight.

Steve Craig, Accused Of Murder, Puts Up A Spectacular Fight To Find The Killer And Clear His Own Name

The Law Comes for Stephen Craig

LIEUTENANT STEPHEN CRAIG, attired in white duty belt and blue serge uniform, leaned against the rail of the U.S.S. Burnham and watched the shore boat come out toward him through the fog.

Steve Craig, at present officer of the deck, was interested in the shore boat only because

The Devil with Wings

by
L. RON HUBBARD

CAPTAIN ITO SHINOHARI
HERO IN KILLING OF
AKUMA-NO-HANÉ

TOKIO, JAPAN—May 9 (Tekko News Agency)—General Ytonho Shimokado, commanding Japanese Imperial Troops at Port Arthur, Manchukuo, announced today that Akuma-no-Hané, infamous white

HURRICANE

by L. RON HUBBARD

Captain Spar, escaped from the mire of a penal colony, sets out to get the man who sent him to hell

On Blazing Wings

The city in the sky was full and bright before him, and he was flying into it

PULPATEER

by L. RON HUBBARD

A COLUMN RECENTLY SHOT ACROSS the United States bringing a hitherto unknown side of pulp writing to light. This choice bit of reporting flowed from the pen of the writer's friend, Mr. Odd McIntyre, and to say the very least, it is very odd.

"A weird offshoot of magazine publishing is evidenced in a 'pulp periodical' factory in New York. A company which publishes a string of cheap fiction thrillers has reduced writing to a fine commercial art. Every possible historic plot has been catalogued, and copies are furnished a group of writers who punch the clock like factory hands.

"There are magazines about the West, the sea, the jungles, etc. At the head of the writing staff there is a sort of city editor who apportions each day's work, telling one to write a sea story, using plot Number 4; another a wild west thriller, plot Number 11; and so on.

"Plots of the world's best literature are so twisted that 'Ivanhoe' becomes 'Rutledge's Red Revenge.' And 'The Merchant of Venice' becomes 'Love in the Jungle.'

"The men work on salary, like newspapermen, and must turn in so many thousands of words a day. Since the plots are furnished, they only want men who are swift in grinding out copy."

Mr. McIntyre is about due for a new espionage staff. The old one he must control is growing rather rusty, training on crude oil or banana oil or something of the sort. Their reports of late have been growing more and more ludicrous.

Recently, Mr. McIntyre stated that the kingpin of the pulps was making thirty thousand a year, a fact which is very interesting and surprising to the kingpin himself who has had to answer many, many embarrassing questions from various sources to eradicate that statement about Arthur J. Burks.

O. O. McIntyre simultaneously fueling a red scare and lambasting pulps in a single furious breath

But never mind, we're thinking about this pulp factory. I have been trying very hard to find out who runs this plant because I would like very much to get into it myself. But evidently Mr. McIntyre has a better source than I have, as I only write for the pulps for a living.

My information must be very limited. In fact I have not written for anybody but the Big Five and the little five and a few others. Dell, Standard, Street and Smith, Munsey, and last but not least, Popular, have seen fit at one time and another to print my stories in any and all lengths covering every angle of the pulp field but the love story. Other, lesser firms have done the same.

Now I am very angry about all this because it seems to me that some of my companies must have been holding out on me. I think that I ought to rate being on a staff which writes to Plot Number 4, 6, or maybe 9. That would be so simple, you see, and I would never have to worry about things like rent and hospital bills and new shoes for the kids. Somebody is obviously holding out on me.

But all foolish remarks to the contrary, I wish all these columnists, in their lofty heights of literarity, would stick to their last. There has been another one of these pulp-attack epidemics going the rounds and it seems to be catching. The American Mercury published a very good article on the subject which was rather true and fair but altogether too bitter.

These things do a pulpateer no little harm. Primarily, a pulpateer is a very decent writer (he has to be that, you know). He is sincere about his work as any of the top rankers will testify. If you should happen to intimate to a pulpateer that his stories are trash, you are likely to be soundly punched in the nose—and rightly. He tries to write his very best and make his stories exciting and often he gets a lot more than excitement into them.

There is no real reason for ignorant people to rip and tear at a man's livelihood and vocation and avocation when it actually means nothing to said people. Such backhanded slaps hurt not a little. The idea that pulp writing is mechanical is already too prevalent.

Here is what such a thing does: A friend of mine, earning his bread by adding figures or fixing streetcars or flying transport planes reads such an article or statement. He does not bother to acquaint himself with the facts any more than the man who wrote the remark did. Instantly, however, this friend of mine says, "So that's what Hubbard is doing. Hell, I thought he was a real writer."

And the next time I see the man he is apt to make some jest concerning my work and he is no longer a friend of mine.

These things put a bar between a pulpateer and the writing world, a bar which really should not exist. In articles, for instance, I often have to interview prominent men in this field and that. In stories I sometimes feel that my information is not quite sound. To give everyone an even break I look up someone who is directly connected with my subject. In explaining myself I say that this will be for "War Birds" or "Adventure" and if he is a reader of magazines in the so-called quality group, or of columns, he is apt to smile at me and tell me, "No thanks, I don't want to appear in such cheap magazines."

That has happened to me before and it will happen again. How can I do a sincere and honest job, for instance, with the Coast Guard under such conditions? And yet the story or article will be read by a hundred thousand or more people who are rather impressionable. If I'm wrong, they get the Coast Guard wrong and then there's a double howl about it.

Outside of losing me friends, demeaning my profession and undermining my sources, the sales of such magazines may be hurt as a consequence. People (although I'm sure I don't know why) believe what they read in the papers.

Such remarks discourage pulp tyros and keep them from a possible living by causing them to write down to their markets.

"If you should happen to intimate to a pulpateer that his stories are trash, you are likely to be soundly punched in the nose..."
L. Ron Hubbard to O. O. McIntyre

In the case of the old dime novel (which Odd McIntyre probably read and enjoyed in his true "homey" style as a kid) it has recently been discovered that the finest sources of Western America as it was lay in these same paper-covered books. The men who wrote those stories were, for the most part, former punchers, sailors, soldiers of fortune and God knows what else. In, for instance, "Colonel Prentiss Ingraham's" LAFITTE'S LIEUTENANT, in his BRAND OF THE RED ANCHOR, I have found a startling knowledge of historical types of vessels, of gunnery, tactics, and costume. I had recourse to such sources while I was writing one called UNDER THE BLACK ENSIGN and I checked Ingraham and found he knew a lot more than I did for all my study.

The dime novel, booed in its day, is now filed carefully in the rare book collection of the Library of Congress.

A surprising number of historical novels, well reviewed when they came out in book form, have appeared serially in pulps. A large number of pulp stories are now carefully bound up in anthologies.

To defame the pulps and the pulpateer seems to be a habit with so-called quality writers, columnists, and novelists. They are in another quite different strata. They talk about something indefinite which they call art and then they sit down to their typewriters and dash out something they read with ecstasy but which may be so faulty that an honest author cringes. Witness, for God's sake, MAN ON THE FLYING TRAPEZE, and then glance through the as yet serial ONE WOMAN ALIVE which takes as its source what a lot of us have been doing for years under the name of pseudo-scientific. More originality has appeared in WEIRD TALES per story than H. G. Wells put into THINGS TO COME.

I could name you scores of famous authors who trained in pulp. Their training must have been sound because their works are sound. Only one detective writer who is now famous scorns the pulps. He never appeared on wood-pulp paper and never tried to read it over. He had the popular touch and he got it second hand from writers who served their 'prenticeship in pulp.

It amuses me to read in McIntyre's column about this man and that, evidently very revered by McIntyre, and then to remember that this man and that came up through rough paper.

To glance over the pulps on the stands you cannot help but remark the names on the covers. If you know anything about pulp you can doubtless recall little bits of this and that man's history.

Pulpateers, columns to the contrary, are an assorted, romantic crew, making their livings with their typewriters and doing very well at it. Right here I really ought to prove this by citing a few cases, but the mere thought makes me recoil. I don't want this to be a book, but an article. These men and women have done everything and anything you can name. Reporters, punchers, detectives, wanderers, professors, sergeants, captains, columnists (beg pardon, Odd), sailors, movie writers, salesmen, city editors, and so on and on and on. One chap I enjoy reading is, to my surprise, a full-fledged general. Another (three in fact) is a Commander of the Legion of Honor. Another has been decorated by two kings. Still another has jumped the ocean twice. One was city ed for an NY daily (his hobby was firing columnists). Another is a civil engineer with years in the tropics to his credit. Another commanded a Turkish division in the World War. Another is a World War ace. But, as I said, I could go on forever.

> *"I could name you scores of famous authors who trained in pulp. Their training must have been sound because their works are sound."*

Now in thinking all this over, doesn't it seem to you that a man who can only mark one track (from his home town to the darkness of a New York apartment) down on his personal map rather sticks his neck into the guillotine when he passes judgment on the work of men, not mice?

There isn't any real reason for such idiotic and erroneous statements which are made without the least effort at verification.

The trouble with these critics seems to be that they stamp out on ground they have never seen.

I venture to say that these critics have never seen a pulp magazine anywhere but on a newsstand. Perhaps it would be educational if they would buy a copy of a pulp and sit themselves down to read it.

There are rotten stories in the pulps, of course, but with great candor I can verify the statement that there are lousy stories in the slicks, in books, and in the little magazines. We do not condemn these three fields in one lump remark. I don't get the point of lumping all pulps and all pulp stories into one great class.

And I don't get the point in running down men who are trying to do a job as well as they can.

As for having Plot 4 and Plot 11 furnished, McIntyre might be a wiser man if he tried to write and sell a pulp story. I doubt that he could. I know dozens of people who are always sidling up to a writer and saying, "I've got a swell plot for you." The plot, I might say, is a very small part of a story. Handling is a fine art and handling determines the yarn from beginning to end.

Please pardon me when I smile a little at Mr. McIntyre's selection of plot sources. "Ivanhoe," according to Scott's own statement is a pulp yarn. The plot of "The Merchant of Venice" had been used several thousand times before Shakespeare ever plagiarized it. You can find both plots in Greek, and in Arabic.

Plot, Mr. McIntyre, is the least of a pulpateer's worries. I have an agent who drowns me in plots I cannot use. I was once given a book which contains millions of plots and I cannot use that either.

I recently saw a pack of cards which dealt of plot but, although they might help somebody they don't help me.

During the past year I sold many hundreds of thousands of words, and I don't happen to be ashamed of any story in the lot. In fact, Mr. McIntyre, I would like to forward you the file for your education. I once gave a college short story professor a twenty thousand worder to read. He had never read a pulp story in his life and yet he was eager to heap sarcasm upon my head. He read this story all right, and it kept him up until dawn. He has had nothing to say about pulp since. Maybe the dose would be good for you, too.

When I look for tripe to read, I don't go to the pulps. I go to the magazine section of the Sunday papers. I think pulpateers avoid that market because the pay is too small and too irregular.

And here is one last, parting shot. I have a few slick paper friends and I've loaned most of them money at one time or another. I don't want anything to do with slick paper...I couldn't write light love and the old trite doctor-in-love plot anyway because it is too bare.

But just by way of proving that pulpateers aren't really machines, I have a couple books on the way up. I'll forward some copies to you. I might as well do something with the books because they certainly won't make over a cent a word even if they happen to become best sellers.

This is a mild protest, I assure you. If at any time you wish to know anything, Mr. McIntyre, about writing and writers, please communicate with some writers for a change.

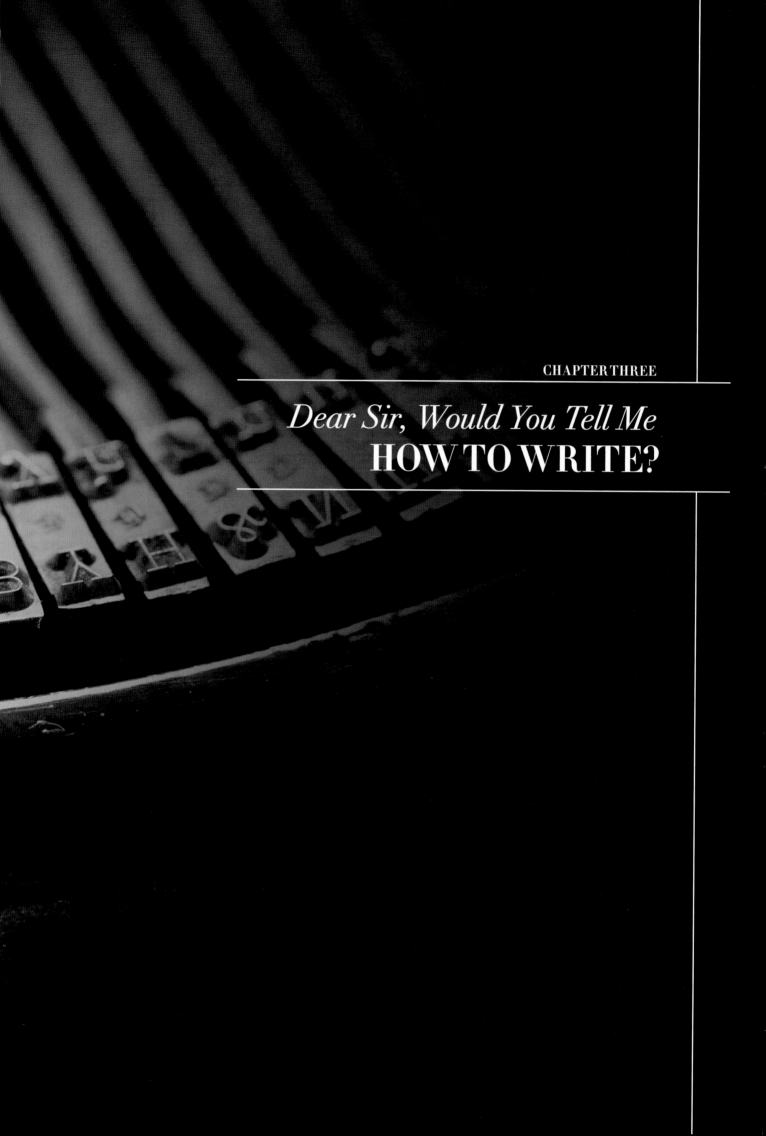

CHAPTER THREE

Dear Sir, Would You Tell Me
HOW TO WRITE?

Dear Sir, Would You Tell Me How to Write?

AMONG OTHER COMMENTS REGULARLY HEARD IN reference to the L. Ron Hubbard of 1935: He possessed a singularly rare concern for those who wished to write yet lacked both editorial direction and contacts. He worked ceaselessly to open traditionally bolted doors of reputable agents and publishers and

otherwise stood ready to help all who harbored the dream of writing for a living. The statements are true, as the letters to follow will attest.

Regarding those letters: while publishers were theoretically open to all submissions, senior editors generally reviewed only those manuscripts of known authors or those offered through agents whom they likewise knew. The catch: one could not enlist an agent unless previously published or at least recommended by an author of repute. In reply, and especially in his capacity as president of American Fiction Guild's New York chapter, LRH fought to admit the unpublished author as a "novice."

Whereupon he would usher them into the rear of Rosoff's Restaurant for those all-important introductions to editors and publishers lunching on club sandwiches.

Offered here is a sampling of the to-and-from novice authors, including an obscure Catherine L. Moore—then employed as a bank secretary, but latterly remembered for a long and distinguished career as a novelist and teleplay writer. Additionally included are Ron's "solid meat" replies to the "word-weary" and his letter from the airwaves of radio KVOO—all in answer to that question of questions: "Would you tell me how to write?" ∎

Rosoff's on West 43rd Street, New York, New York: primary watering hole for the American Fiction Guild and occasional meeting ground for writers and editors lunching on a "horrible slice of ham with a pineapple ring"

Dear Mr. Hubbard;

For a long time I have been writing fiction. Most of it came back and lies neglected in my files along with letters from editors and plain rejects.

I have not managed to sell a single line. Of course I had some published in the school paper and a few places like that but I think that if I could get at it right I could earn a good living by writing.

The man down at the service station has read a lot of my stories and has given me quite a lot of good advice on them. He took a writing course, I think, or maybe it was journalism, at the local university.

Is it asking too much for you to answer this question? How did you start to write and sell?

Respectfully,
Jim Higgins

Dear Higgins;

It isn't a question of *how* I started to write, it's a question of *why*.

There's a world of difference there. I take it that you have a job, otherwise you wouldn't eat and if you don't eat, you don't last long.

We assume, therefore, that you are eating. That is bad, very bad. No man who wants to start writing should be able to eat regularly. Steaks and potatoes get him out of trim.

When a man starts to write, his mental attitude should be one of anguish. He *has* to sell something because he *has* to pay the grocery bill.

My advice to you is simple. If you have the idea that you can write saleable stuff, go off someplace and get short of money. You'll write it all right, and what's more you'll sell it.

Witness the case of a lady I know in New York. She was plugging at writing for some fifteen years without selling a line. She left the Big Town with her husband. In the Pacific Northwest her husband died and left her stranded.

She went to work in a lumber mill and wrote a book about it and sold it first crack out. She worked as a waitress and wrote a book about that and sold it.

Having succeeded with two books, she went back to the Big Town and got herself a job in the library until the returns came in. She wrote all the time after that but she was eating. In sawmill and hash house she wasn't living comfortably. She needed the extra.

She hasn't sold a line since.

The poet in the garret is not a bad example, after all. Personally I write to pay my bills.

Jack London, I am told, plastered his bills over his writing desk and every time he wanted to get up or go arty he glanced at them and went right on grinding it out.

I think if I inherited a million tomorrow my stuff would go esoteric and otherwise blah.

I started to write because I had come back from the West Indies where I had been hunting gold and discovered that we had a depression going on up here. I had to start eating right away.

Jack London

I started writing one story a day for six weeks. I wrote that story in the afternoon and evening. I read the mag I was to make the next day before I went to bed. I plotted the yarn in my sleep, rose and wrote it, read another mag all the way through, went to bed.........

Out of that month and a half of work I have sold fiction to the sum of nine hundred dollars. At the end of the six weeks I received checks amounting to three hundred and two dollars and fifty cents.

Unable to stand prosperity I left for California. I got broke there, wrote for a month without stopping to breathe, sold eleven hundred dollars worth.

Nothing like necessity to take all this nonsense about how you ought to reform editors right out of your head.

As far as that guy down at the service station is concerned, he may be okay, but remember this: You are the writer. You have to learn your own game. And if he's never hit the bread and butter side of the business, he knows less about it than you do, all courses to the contrary.

Write me again when you've gone and done some tall starving.

Best regards,
L. Ron Hubbard

Dear Mr. Hubbard;

I have always felt that I could write if I tried, but somehow I've been so busy during the last few years that I haven't had much chance.

I was married when I was very young and every time I started my writing, Joe would either move (Joe is my husband) or we'd have to both work because of the bills.

Most of my children have grown up now to a point where they can take care of themselves and although I have some time now I don't seem to be able to get down to work. I have a lot of stories in the back of my head but I just can't find time or ways and means of getting them down on paper. I feel that this is mostly mental.

Would you tell me how you write?

Wishfully,
Mary Stein

Dear Mary Stein;

Remember when you read this that I didn't ask to be appointed your psycho-analyst. I am nothing but a hard-working writer, after all, using fictitious characters and working them over. When real people get planted in front of me I stand back and gape and wonder if it can be true.

Let me tell you about Margaret Sutton. She writes some of the best children's books being written today. She has five kids, I think. A lot of them need plenty of attention. She has to support them and do her own work and everything.

One day somebody asked her why she didn't get a maid now she had so much royalty money. She blinked and said, "A maid? Why, what would I do with my extra time?"

Well, there you have it. Maybe it *is* mental.

From Crabtown to Timbuktu, when I have been introduced as a writer, somebody always has said, "Well, now, I could write too if I just had some time."

That is a queer mental quirk with people. If a man is a writer, he is doing something everybody thinks they can do. A chap who is the head of a big insurance company, highly successful, once said to me, "I would like to write, but I never seem to be able to find the time."

It's their way of apology, I guess. Nearly everyone makes that remark and, to be brutally frank, it is a source of much merriment in the professional ranks.

I am not one to talk about working and writing in the same breath. I have a law around the house here which says that writing comes first and to hell with everything else. The lawn grows into an alfalfa field, the pipes drip merrily, the floors need paint, but I turn a deaf ear to pleas and go right on writing.

I have found this to be the case. My time at the typewriter is worth, per hour, what the average artisan gets per week. I do not work the same hours he does. I work far less, but I work much harder.

Therefore I paint my floors and fix my pipes with the typewriter keys, if you get me. One short story will pay for all the work to be done around this house in a month including the maid's wages.

People let petty things keep them away from a typewriter. I think that is true because they *want* to be kept away from the machine. When you start to write there seems to be an invisible wall separating you from the keyboard. Practice is the only thing which will dissipate it.

If you make yourself write during trying times, you are doing a lot toward whipping your jinx.

Recently I was very ill in a New York apartment. My agent, Ed Bodin, and his wife came in.

They left at 8:45 P.M. They returned at 11:30. In the interim I had grown restless. I felt that I was stale, would be unable to write anything for months. Then I got mad at such a traitorous thought, climbed out of bed, sat down at the mill and wrote a story which I gave to Ed upon his return.

I knew, of course, that the story would be rotten. Half the time I couldn't see the paper, I was so dizzy.

But I guess I was wrong. Ed sold it almost immediately to DETECTIVE FICTION WEEKLY. It was "The Mad Dog Murders."

My contention is that, if you have the stuff on the ball, you can write anytime, anyplace and anything.

Best regards,
L. Ron Hubbard

Right Detective Fiction Weekly, featuring hard-boiled tales of gumshoes and dames

SEPT. 12
10¢

Exciting Mysteries

DETECTIVE
FICTION WEEKLY
Formerly FLYNN'S

The Gleeful Gunman

Bucks the Toughest
Cop Ever Born—*by*

Johnston McCulley

L. Ron Hubbard
Fred MacIsaac
Norbert Davis
Earl W. Scott

Dear Mr. Hubbard;

I been pounding out a lot of western yarns and shipping same to certain editors located in New York where the only horse in town is located on a whiskey bottle.

These gents claim, per letter and returned stories, that I haven't got any real feel of the West.

The same irritates me considerable. I spotted a yarn of yours and you seemed to know hosses hands down and guns likewise and that don't measure like most of these western yarns.

I think maybe I better go back to wranglin' hosses because maybe I don't know how to put it in stories, I sure do know something about putting them in corrals.

I thought it was about time somebody wrote some western stories that knew what they was writing about. I still think so.

The question is, what the hell can I do about it?

Yours truly,
Steed Monahan

Dear Steed Monahan;

You have laid the finger on something. I'm not sure what. I wouldn't go as far as to say that you have the dope but lack the knack of writing fiction. You know there might be something in that. Anyway, I'm no judge because I never read any of your stuff.

This question once leaped up at a New York Chapter meeting of the American Fiction Guild. Clee Woods, Al Echols, Sayer, and maybe Tom Roan got pretty deep into the argument about whether or not you had to know the West to write westerns.

I wasn't so very interested because my forte is adventure and such, but I listened because I had been raised in Montana but had never been able to sell a good western story.

These lads who knew the West had it all settled to their satisfaction that you had to have the dope and data before you could put down the words and syllables.

Then Frank Gruber stood up and said he'd sold a few westerns that year. Fifteen or so. And that was odd because, he said, he had never been closer to a ranch than editing a chicken paper in the Middle West.

So there you are. The dope and data does not outweigh good story writing. I can write stories about pursuit pilots, stories about coal miners, stories about detectives, stories about public enemies, G-men, arctic explorers, Chinese generals, etc.

Which doesn't mean that I had to shoot down another plane to get the dope. I have never: 1. Been in a coal mine. 2. Been a detective. 3. A public enemy. 4. Been a G-man. 5. Explored the Arctic. 6. Been a Chinese general.

And yet I am proud of a record which was only marred by one inaccuracy in a story, and that very trivial. By getting experience somewhere near the field, I can exploit the field.

For instance, of late, I have been looking into dangerous professions. I've climbed sky-scrapers with steeplejacks, dived with deep-sea divers, stunted with test pilots, and made faces at lions. But at no time was I actually a member of that particular profession of which I was to write. I didn't have to be because the research enabled me to view it from a longer, more accurate range.

The only thing you can do is try hard to write a swell, fast action western yarn. Peddle it to every western book in the field. Ask for some honest comments on it.

Under the Die-Hard Brand: a classic Wild West yarn from an L. Ron Hubbard who actually knew of what he wrote

But before you do this, be sure you are writing what these magazines are buying.

A good story comes first. Information comes second. An editor of one of our best books recently told me, "Accuracy be damned. Very few gentlemen will know you're wrong. Give us the story. We can buy the accuracy from a twenty-five a week clerk with a library card. You don't have to *know*. You can *write*."

Ride 'em, cowboy, and don't pull any leather until they spot your trouble for you. But if you can't write, you can't write, no matter how much you know.

And I guess that's all I know about that subject.

Best regards,
L. Ron Hubbard

Dear Mr. Hubbard;

During the last few months I have managed to sell some of my stories to magazines located in New York. I have every assurance that I can keep right on selling these stories of mine and I think it's about time I made a break for the Big Town.

I've been reading the writer's magazines and I think you have to know all about New York and the markets before you can really get places in this game.

I've been making over a hundred dollars a month in the writing game. I asked one of the editors about this and he told me by all means look him up when I got to New York. As that sounds encouraging, I'm planning on leaving.

Jeb wants me to go with him to Baffin Land on his whaler this summer, but I think I better give my writing a break and go to New York instead.

But I thought, before I made a decision, I'd better write to some professional writer like you who's been in New York a lot and ask him what conditions were there.

My stories are mostly about this part of the world as I am always cruising around or trekking off someplace with guys like Jeb, or Carlson (he's the Mounty here), but I think I ought to have a wider field for my work. Detective stories, for instance and things like that.

Would you tell me about New York?

Sincerely,
Arch Bankey

⌖

Dear Arch Bankey;

A few years ago I knew a beachcomber in Hong Kong. All he ever talked about was the day he would go to New York. That was the place. New York!

But he was smarter than the rest of us. He never went. He just talked about it.

There's nothing like knowing your editors, of course. Editors are swell people as a rule. Nothing like getting their slant face to face. Increase your sales no end.

But if you think you can go to New York and live there on a hundred a month, you're as crazy as a locoed wolf. Think about it from this angle:

In New York you'll have noise, bad living conditions, and higher expenses. You will have to keep right on writing to keep eating.

You are used to writing where the biggest noise is a pine tree shouting at its neighbor. That is the condition you know. You can write there.

Chances are a hundred to one that you won't be able to turn out a line when the subway begins to saw into your nerves, when the L smashes out your eardrums overhead, when ten thousand taxi drivers clamp down on their horns.

If you can't write, you can't eat because you won't have enough reserve.

Besides, the markets you mention are not very reliable. Those eds are the brand that wants something for nothing. Wait until you sell the big books in the pulp field. Wait until you crack into at least four of the big five publishing houses. Wait until you are pretty sure you know what you're doing in the game before you make a change.

I've wrecked myself time after time with changes just because I have itchy feet. I have just come from New York. I got along all right, for a very little while, then the town got me. I had a big month and managed to get out.

But once New York gets you, you're got.

Some of the swellest guys I know are in New York. Also some of the worst heels.

Here's my advice, take it for what it's worth to you.

Jeb and the whaler will provide you with lots of story

Waldorf-Astoria

material. Go with him and write it. Trek out with that Mounty and study the way he goes about it. Take your trips with your eyes open for data.

Neither Jeb nor Carlson will let you starve. If you can't put out the wordage, you'll find editors far from interested in you.

Write everything you can, study the mags you're sending stuff to, collect every scrap of story material. Collect yourself checks to the amount of one thousand dollars no more no less. With that all in one piece, shove off for New York.

On arrival get yourself the best clothes you can buy. Register at the Waldorf-Astoria. Take editors out to lunch in a Cadillac taxi.

Stay in New York until all you've got left is your return trip ticket. Pack up and leave right away quick for home.

Don't try to work in New York. Don't try to make it your home. Go there with a roll and do the place right, then grab the rattler for Hudson Bay before the glamor wears off.

Sitting in a shabby room, pounding a mill with the landlady pounding on the door is fine experience, but I think gunning for whales up off Baffin Land is much more to your liking.

Best regards,
L. Ron Hubbard

170 King Street

North Bay, Ontario

29th May 1936

Mr. L. Ron Hubbard

40 King Street

New York City, N.Y.

Dear Mr. Hubbard,

Received your very generous letter in answer to my query. I feel I cannot let it pass without letting you know how much I appreciate the trouble you took to inform me about things I couldn't have known otherwise, or without wasting a good deal of time, effort and perhaps money. A three-page letter packed full of meat of the kind I've been wanting is what I got. Thanks to you, I'm going at the writing game much less blindly with regard to trying to hit markets, and with a good deal more confidence. To show you there IS a great disadvantage in being away from the hub of things, it's taken me nearly four years of blind groping to get the sort of stuff you've handed me from your experience as a writer that has arrived. I'm not likely to forget you took the trouble to grind out three pages of that experience, when honestly I expected a terse reply, if any at all. And that cynical attitude is largely the result of accumulated rejection slips, which in turn, in many cases were the result of not knowing the ropes.

Yours sincerely,

Gordon Walsh

Left New York Harbor; photograph by L. Ron Hubbard

Dear Mr. Hubbard:

I suppose you're wondering of all things, how in the dickens did I ever get hold of your address. Well, it's all pretty simple, when you stop to figure it out. The fact of the matter is, I had occasion to drop in on Ed Bodin, your agent. Naturally, we drifted into conversation. Fell to talking of things pretty general, when all of a sudden: "What's become of Ron Hubbard?" I said. Just like that. I wish you could have seen his face. "Ron Hubbard?" he smiled back at me. "Why, haven't you heard? Hubbard's out in Hollywood." I stared at him a moment in surprise. "Out in Hollywood!" I exclaimed. "This is the first time I've heard of that." "Why, sure," he went on. "Hubbard's got a ten-week contract with the COLUMBIA PICTURE people. He's doing the continuity of a serial for them."

And that's that! Boy, am I glad! Truthfully, if you were my own brother—my own flesh and blood—I couldn't feel more elated. You know how some things just naturally give one a great big thrill? Well, that's just the way this joyful news affected me. "Why the hero worship," you say? Oh, this hero worship of mine—if you may choose to call it such—isn't so hard to explain, Mr. Hubbard. It's founded upon some pretty good substantial reasons. One mighty good reason I might mention right offhand is that I enjoy your stories. You're a dandy good writer. You can be depended upon to turn out interesting story material.

However, it isn't because of this one fact alone—that I enjoy your stories—that I have such a great feeling of admiration and liking for you. There is something else. This something I speak of, has more to do with you as an—INDIVIDUAL. It is a something I believe to be inherent in your nature. Do you know what this something is? It's your—HUMANNESS.

Columbia Pictures, Hollywood, California, where Ron sojourned through the summer of 1937 transforming his novel *Murder at Pirate Castle* into a fifteen-part matinee, *The Secret of Treasure Island*

Here's where you shine, Ron Hubbard. You delight in giving the other fellow a lift up. A little better realization and understanding of the pure joy of living. How do I know? Why, I've experienced it. Do you think I've forgotten how kind you were to me at some of those WRITERS GUILD meetings? I must have bored you to death. However, this didn't faze you; not one iota. There you were, listening to me with all the tolerance and sympathy in the world... More power to YOU! How can a fellow do otherwise than wish such a man as YOU success in any new venture.

Frankly, my one sincere hope is that they sign you up in this picture game at an enormous salary for the rest of your whole natural life...

Very Sincerely Yours,
James F. Ayres

St. Francis Hotel
5533 Hollywood Blvd.
Hollywood, Calif.
June 28, 1937

Dear Ayres;

Your letter was quite a pleasing surprise. I have been wondering what markets you were hitting by this time.

You give me very sparse data about yourself. Are you rolling them steadily? And if so, for whom? Pardon my ignorance but I haven't had time to even look at a magazine for months.

You wish me a most horrible fate in your last line. I'll be very happy to get out of this town. A good pulpateer can make more money in his own markets with the same amount of work. That sounds odd, but then I never work fourteen hours a day on my own stories. Seven days a week. It's more like four hours a day four days a week.

I have finished my original job and now I'm waiting for a report and filling in the time turning out some other stories and getting them into the studios. In addition to this work I have managed to write several novelettes in the past six weeks and as a consequence my energy is at a very low ebb.

Art Burks and George Bruce are out here but I see very little of Bruce. Art and I get together two or three times a week and swear at the movies. Here's wishing you lots of sales.

Best regards,
L. Ron Hubbard

Catherine Moore
2547 Brookside Parkway, South Drive
Indianapolis, Indiana

July 14, 1937

Dear Ron Hubbard:

If it really were an ivory tower in which your letter reached me I'd probably have answered it much sooner. It's been more like an ivory madhouse since my return from California, and though I've been home two weeks I'm not entirely unpacked even yet, which should give you some idea.

Were you in Hollywood at the same time I was? And one of the many interesting people Forrest told me I was missing by leaving for San Francisco so soon? If so I'm awfully disappointed and can only look forward to next fall and your possible trip East, which I hope nothing interferes with. The nice lady of the secondhand magazine shop has written me since you did, sketching a personality that I certainly don't want to miss—one to match your hair, she implies.

I bought FIVE NOVELS several days ago, and last night finally succeeded in finding time to read your "Dive Bomber"—which, I noted with vicarious pride, had first place in the magazine. And I'm pleased and flattered, but not convinced, by the suggestion that our writing is similar. Your taste is so much better than mine. I mean, your very vivid and colorful descriptions come in small doses, instead of encrusting the story so thickly that one's slightly sick from the richness by the time the tale's finished. My stories are like making a meal off chocolate pie and plum pudding, while yours have a sufficient admixture of rare beef-steak and beer and salad to make the dessert welcome instead of cloying.

I think I've come to a crossroads so far as my fantastic writing is concerned. Looking back, I itch for a blue pencil. So much of it would be so much better if a lot of the rococo were cut out. I write in iambic pentameter, for one thing, and too much prose poetry is too much. You've got a feeling of sustained rhythm in your own writing which happily stops short of the sing-song, as mine so often and so unfortunately doesn't. When I have evolved through morasses of over-writing and wordiness and rococo into something approaching what I want to be like, I think the finished product will be very like your own style. Restrained and succinct, yet capable of brief and vivid descriptions all the more vivid for their brevity. Like a couple of lines in a poem I'm fond of, describing a Japanese print, "The skill to do more—With the will to refrain."

Your advice about breaking into other markets than fantasy is one I'm trying to follow, so far without success. I have so little time to write, and so many things to be done in that spare time after working hours, and I'm so lazy anyhow, that somehow I don't seem to get much done. Otis Kline is tutoring me, and with his help maybe the day will come when I can expand a bit in my markets. Meanwhile your encouragement helps a lot. With your experience you should know what you're talking about, and I'm extremely flattered and pleased.

Do you really like writing for a living? You must have bad times when you can't write anything. Doesn't it scare you? Or perhaps you have a separate income. Of course it's a comfort to have a steady job such as mine, with salary coming in whether my mind's a blank or not, but I certainly haven't much time to write. What I need, of course, is someone to stand over me with a long whip to raise a welt on me every time the typewriter lags.

Well, I've a passionate longing to visit Sweden—can't imagine why—so maybe that will prove an incentive. Anyhow, I'll keep your letter and read it over at low ebbs for encouragement.

I am much awed by the fact that you were writing a movie. Was it your first? Why did you have to go to Hollywood to do it? How'd you get the chance? And how badly do you expect to get gypped? I've always heard that unless you're someone like—Oh, Wodehouse or Galsworthy or somebody—you could just expect to be wretchedly underpaid and miserably treated and brazenly pirated if you write for the movies. I have an aunt and an uncle both of whom did a bit of scenario writing years ago, with all the above results. But maybe the Hollywood morals have improved since. Reading over the above, I realize it's somewhat on the order of the famous—"So the wolf left Little Red Riding Hood lying in a pool of blood, torn limb from limb...good *ni-i-ight* kiddies, sweet dreams!" I didn't really mean to paint the picture in such horrid colors, and doubtless you know much more about it than I do. I hope you can dispel my nightmarish impressions and tell me that all is sweetness and light at Columbia Pictures.

I'm on the lookout for BUCKSKIN BRIGADES, which sounds very pleasant. It's going to be fun reading more of your work—I like it very much indeed.

Have you an agent? And what do you really want to do—write novels, or for the movies, or for the slicks, or what? How do you intend to go about working toward the desired end? I wouldn't hesitate to ask questions for fear of being thought inquisitive, of course. You seem to be at the place I hope to reach in a few years—writing widely for the pulps, with a book or two out, beginning to cast glances into the greener pastures beyond. And any technical advice you can give me will be deeply appreciated.

Anyhow, thanks a great deal for all the encouragement, and for liking my gilded-gingerbread style of writing.[*]

Gratefully,
Catherine Moore

[*] *Although an extended search reveals no further LRH-Moore correspondence, we know their friendship had been lengthy—moreover, and notwithstanding her "gilded-gingerbread style," Ms. Moore went on to enjoy a profitable career as both an author of science fiction and a regular contributor to the 1960s hit television series, 77 Sunset Strip.*

KVOO

PHILTOWER · TULSA

Feb. 21, 1938

Mr. L. Ron Hubbard
Western Story Magazine
Street & Smith, Inc.
New York, N.Y.

Dear Mr. Hubbard,

Thursdays at 10:00 P.M., Central Time, I am doing a program called "Writers and Readers" in which is a department called "The Story Behind The Story." Would you send me the "inside" of one of your stories? Notes on the birth of the idea, speed or slowness of sale, technical notes. What any writer wonders about the other guy's story. If you will send me publication date, I'll match the broadcast date and make it a tie-up. We can be heard all over the country at night.

My aim is to publicize the pulps and their writers, and, if even in a small way, make the field greener for us who are feeding in it.

Whatever biographical notes you send with the above will be used.

Cordially,
Bob De Haven
Announcer

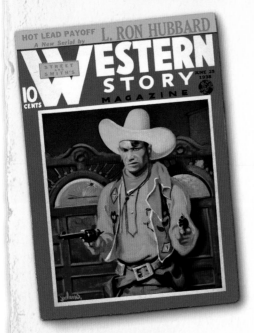

Western Story regularly featured L. Ron Hubbard tales of lone gunslingers "who figured they'd been pushed enough"

The Most Powerful Station between St. Louis, Dallas and Denver

OWNED AND OPERATED BY SOUTHWESTERN SALES CORPORATION
EDWARD PETRY AND CO., INC. NATIONAL REPRESENTATIVES

Bob De Haven
March 10, 1938

WRITERS AND READERS

Good evening, writers and readers, this is Bob De Haven with the Writers and Readers program. What is it? Well, a chat about the great game of putting words into print for entertainment and a chat of interest to those behind as well as in front of the magazines, books and pictures.

Tonight we have the story behind the story contributed by L. Ron Hubbard who writes from the Knickerbocker Hotel in New York. Heaven only knows where he is now. First I'll get you acquainted with Hubbard before going into his story which is on the stands now in Street & Smith's *Western Story* magazine.

Hubbard was born in Nebraska and moved to Oklahoma at the age of three weeks, moved in with his grandfather, Lafe Waterbury, who had an outfit near Durant. Eventually he went to Montana, where the war took his father away in the navy and L. Ron spent years tagging his father around the world.

With his father and independently, L. Ron Hubbard had traveled a quarter of a million miles at nineteen years, through Asia, South Pacific and South America. He then stopped trying to be a civil engineer and tried to be a pilot. He searched for gold in Latin America, ran an expedition and started to write while trailing around the globe. He has sold one of every type of story printed. His published word total is about a million and a half.

His last book was called *Buckskin Brigades*.

So with that introduction let's turn to his story behind the story. It has been on the stands this past week in *Western Story* magazines, the lead story called

"Six-Gun Caballero." It was written several months ago and he says the details are hard to recall because a story written, to him, exists as an individual piece of work and he can't remember a time when it was not written. But he does recall every move that his principal character, Michael Patrick Obañon, made in "Six-Gun Caballero." He came alive before the story started through the typewriter. Hubbard would know him anywhere.

This sounds like characters haunt him and that's right. One character haunted him for four and a half years and made his life miserable. In truth, he was a ghost, this character. He was an ugly fellow who had a habit of vanishing in a puff of smoke and shooting men in the back. This character was developed about five years ago when Hubbard sat down to see if he could write a story in ten days, a full book of 60,000 words. He made it in eleven days and called the book *Pirate Castle*. In it was a pirate's ghost called the Shark of the Caribbean, the villain of the piece, and it was the shark who haunted the author.

And it was annoying in more ways than one to Hubbard—the novel started to collect rejects in wholesale lots. It went to every magazine that ever printed such stories. It went to every publishing house. It went over the Atlantic and had tiffin with London publishers, and even said skoal with the Scandinavians. But to no avail. Nobody wanted that book, and the ghost kept coming back to bother Hubbard in his sleep.

Well—finally one of the major Hollywood studios bought it and hired the author to write the play, and even then, he wasn't through with it. *Argosy* asked for a rewrite of the novel, a change of editors and another request for a rewrite. Finally the story was buried with honor and lives on the screen.

Back to "Six-Gun Caballero." John Burr is *Western Story*'s editor now and Hubbard admits he has a lot of faith in him. He doesn't get sudden spasms like other editors; all he wants is a good story. It doesn't matter what happens as long as the story will interest the reader. That is sensible editing.

Don Michael, for instance, is not the usual western gunman hero at all but a very smooth lad. That made the story and that is why people will read it. Often, even in a slick paper, an editor will get a formula he likes and then every writer has to adhere to that formula—which drives most any writer into madness.

When I asked L. Ron Hubbard what kind of a fellow is the average writer, he refused to be trapped. Very seldom are they college graduates. Rich man, poor man, beggarman and thief, since O. Henry did time in Ohio, even if there were very extenuating circumstances. That's what makes the game interesting. From one day to another, no editor knows from whence the best story of the year will spring. Editors depend on old-timers, but then writing is a trade as much as plumbing. It has to be learned by practice.

L. Ron Hubbard says a writer's success is his ability to get drunk—on words. And here's good advice, kind listeners, the more a writer writes, the more he can write. Hubbard says if he does five thousand words today, he can do ten thousand tomorrow. But if he stops for a week it takes another week to get going again. A writer can write himself into a jag of weeks duration. Hubbard recently did one hundred and thirty thousand words in six days. He mentions Arthur J. Burks as a real speed demon on a typewriter. Burks recently wrote 70,000 words in three days. Quality seems to improve with speed.

"Six-Gun Caballero" was done in five days. Five thousand the first day, something like a thousand each of the next three days and twelve thousand the last day.

Well, thanks many times to L. Ron Hubbard. Read his "Six-Gun Caballero" and express your thanks by telling his editor what you think of the yarn. The interest of these top-notchers is greatly appreciated.

Well, writers and readers, our time is really short. Next week we'll be on at 10:00 P.M. and at the same time on succeeding weeks. Come early…stay late… This is Bob De Haven hoping you'll listen again and tell your friends about this program.

Tulsa, Oklahoma

Commissioner Valentine

Among other duties incumbent upon an American Fiction Guild president was the enlistment of speakers for the Friday night gatherings in the lounge of the Hotel Knickerbocker.

In addition to this Commissioner Valentine, the Guild had previously hosted the New York City coroner (who discussed death from strangulation) and a Marquis de la Falaise de la Coudray, recently returned from a photo safari across Indochina tiger country. The point: apart from Arthur Burks (a former Marine from the Nicaraguan bush), Dashiell Hammett (a former Pinkerton detective) and the famously adventuring L. Ron Hubbard himself, few members of that Guild actually knew of what they wrote. Hence, enlightening talks from those who haunted grisly realms. ■

AMERICAN FICTION GUILD
40 KING STREET
NEW YORK CITY

November 23, 1935

Commissioner Valentine
Police Department
New York City

Dear Sir:

The New York Chapter of the American Fiction Guild is holding an informal dinner meeting at the Hotel Knickerbocker December 6, Friday evening at six-thirty.

At the meetings it is customary to have some noted personality of the day address the professional writers of the organization upon some subject touching their work. We have had, for instance, in the past, several noted criminologists whose talks have been of great help to our detective story writers, most of whom try in all sincerity to present the police departments accurately in their stories.

It has been suggested that you might like to deliver your views with regard to the problem of crime. It would not, I assure you, fall on barren ground. Our detective writers reach between fifteen and twenty million impressionable minds a month and it has often been mentioned that fiction might do well to play a hand with the law. Crime stories have always borne the brunt of many attacks, and it is conceivable that they influence crime itself. So far, however, the law itself has done little but condemn detective fiction.

Very few of our detective writers—and by that I mean some of the biggest names in such fiction—have ever seen the inside of a station house. Most of this material is turned out blind. The writers do not seem to realize that they hold a mighty bludgeon of influence with their stories.

While the police departments are critical of newspapers and pay strict attention to newspaper comment, these departments pay little attention to fiction which ranks only second in importance to newspapers.

The fault does not lie wholly with the writers. They do not think that police stations and police agents have time to give out accurate information concerning their work and, as a consequence, the detective writer has molded a model of his own which is quite probably far from the truth.

Recently we considered asking James J. Finn of the Hauptmann case to speak at one of our future meetings, but in discussing detective work we decided that we might make an attempt to better the position of our detective writers.

We know that you are given more than you can possibly do, we appreciate that your time is valuable and that this request might seem a little presumptuous, but there is this to consider: If you, with your position and authority, spoke to us in regard to police work, and extended to our detective writers an invitation to help the law with their work, and if you were to suggest that any station house and precinct was open to their inspection, we are certain that the address would have a greatly desired effect.

You would not, in extending that invitation, deluge your department with any amount of work. There are less than a hundred detective writers of importance in the country. A large share of them will be present at the dinner. But though their numbers are few, this scant hundred write ninety-five percent of all the detective fiction printed in the country, from the best selling novel down to the cheapest detective pulp.

It is, therefore, a rather simple task to influence the entire field. Fiction has made the G-man soar to heroic heights in the hands of this group of writers. It was this which suggested to us that we might better our treatment on a closer subject, the police departments of our large cities.

The American Fiction Guild operates primarily for the benefit of today's professional writer, but sometimes we step aside and grasp other urgent work. We fight plagiarism, fraud of all kinds, and so you might say that we're something of a police department ourselves.

Any message you might care to give the New York Chapter of this organization would be relayed promptly to almost every writer of importance in the United States.

We want, frankly, a closer alliance between fiction and fact. We have accomplished that in other fields. The Department of Justice has given writers immeasurable aid so that G-man fiction is gradually becoming accurate and there is, therefore, a better public understanding of that work.

This is, therefore, no idle request that we make. We earnestly desire your presence at this dinner. It is not exactly a social affair and it does not try to achieve social standing. We are men trying to do a sincere job in a sometimes difficult world. Our imaginations give us worldly wealth and information is highly responsible for whatever prestige we might attain. An Address by you and an invitation from you would result, we assure you, in mutual benefit.[*]

Respectfully,

L. Ron Hubbard

---

[*] *Although no record of Commissioner Valentine's address appears in the pages of the American Fiction Guild Bulletin, more than one author of detective mysteries was soon turning up with lists of questions for New York Police Department officers.*

Right Thrilling Detective, featuring Ron's unforgettable
tale of zombie murders, *Dead Men Kill*

THRILLING

DETECTIVE

10¢

JULY

ALL STORIES COMPLETE

MARGIE
HARRIS

C. K. M.
SCANLON

HAROLD
DE POLO

Featuring:
**DEAD MEN
KILL**
A Complete
Book-Length Novel
By L. RON HUBBARD

CRIME MUST GO
By
NORMAN A. DANIELS

Literature for Breakfast

Quite apart from all else Ron championed in the name of truly popular literature, we come upon his modest proposal to the Kellogg Company. Then (as now) synonymous with Corn Flakes, the Kellogg's box, indeed, stood on every typical American breakfast table, while heroic ballads penned in Tin Pan Alley continued to capture the popular imagination. As for his suggestion regarding American presidents and a "classical series," it just so happens munching Americans would eventually find something very similar on their cereal boxes. ∎

L. Ron Hubbard
Route One—Box 452
Port Orchard, Washington

General Manager
THE KELLOGG COMPANY
Battle Creek, Mich.

Dear Sir;

For many a year I have been grossly annoyed by the packaging proclivities of the manufacturers of prepared cereals and, I have reason to believe, I am only one among millions with the same complaint.

However, it has always been a maxim of mine never to criticize unless something better can be suggested. Accordingly, I generated an idea which might or might not be of interest to you.

Every morning, millions of Americans groggily seat themselves at their breakfast tables and stare stupidly at the cereal box while stoking themselves with the contents. The cereal box is the fixture of the breakfast table and ranks with ham and eggs in Americanism. But when the consumer begins to imbibe the contents he is also imbibing the intelligence printed upon the box. He reads everything on it. Because it is the brightest thing on the table it commands and gets his attention even though it has nothing to either show or say beyond the lauding of the contents. As the consumer is already oversold on everything under the sun, he cares very little about the advertising.

Some time ago—and perhaps still—you ran a sort of continued story on one of your cereal boxes. But this was a rather wide idea because it is a long time between boxes. Then you had some very short sketches of this and that, but these too were most inadequate.

You labor under the fixation that only children eat cereal and so you plaster the box with sub-child objects. It is to be doubted if children form a fifth of the consumers of prepared cereals, and, even if you must still slant toward the child, you can bracket the work to miss the elder eater less widely.

To the point then: you should have something which bears repetitious inspection. Neither continued story, short story nor the lives of great men can answer this test. Once read they are finished and, when the consumer must read them three mornings in a row, they are irksome. Especially are they a source of annoyance to the elder on the third morning because, initially, they were designed wholly for children.

The problem lies mainly in the fact that the box must carry the name and advertising of the cereal with due attention to recipes and what one gets by sending in a box top and ten cents. But this can be circumnavigated handsomely by using a method hitherto unused on any package, so far as I know.

Oil paper used to furnish the outer wrapper of the package. This has now been driven inside, for the most part. But, supposing that you wished to ingratiate your cereal with the most irritable of eaters, how could you avoid placing all the lurid advertising before his fastidious but uncontrollable eyes and still give your package adequate display on the grocer's shelves, if not through the medium of this exterior wrapper? If the inner package contained the cereal's name and the name of its manufacturer in letters only twelve point, they would still be read and received by the consumer at his breakfast—in fact they would be better received.

The box, as it is now presented, could be the same box in appearance on the grocer's shelves with only a slight difference and certainly at no cost greater than its advertising value, if all present matter was printed upon a semi-transparent outer cover which could be removed before the box reached the breakfast table. The box itself, in this case, would then carry, in addition to what follows, the name of the cereal and its manufacturer to ensure their being remembered.

Now, for the new box, the face of which would very dimly show through the outside wrapper, there are innumerable things which could be used which would have appeal both to children and elders. The main thing is to make the box so very attractive that it will be a distinct addition to the appearance of the breakfast table so that mama would never forbear to place it boldly thereon—a thing which esthetic mamas do not very often do in the box's present condition.

Once there was an excuse for lurid packaging. Inks and printing methods outlawed any great attempt at handsome presentation. But now, with the improved methods of multicolor printing, when many can be placed at the same time in their exact shades, it becomes possible to cheaply achieve very beautiful results.

First, there could be ballads. There are hundreds and hundreds of them in existence, all of them public property by now. Men always wish, covertly or otherwise, that they knew a string of ballads. However, it is rare to find even an accurate printing of even the most famous of them. "Young Charlotte," "Jesse James," "Casey Jones," "Springfield Mountain," "The Face on the Barroom Floor," and a thousand others are in current knowledge, *but* few are the people who have read all of them or any of them. On the shelf, the housewife finds the old, familiar package, somewhat changed by the box printing which barely shows through. She buys, as usual, but when she gets home she tears off the printed translucent wrapper and finds something worth looking at.

In colorful modern watercolor there are the pertinent scenes in "Casey Jones" or "The Highwayman" or some similar piece. Then, spaced to run on the four sides in order are the verses of the ballad, running around and about the pictures. The kids are entranced. They've never dreamed that any such rhyme existed and they go to school and play highwayman or railroad engineer. Papa always had a sneaking hunch he'd like to know that thing and so, there he sits, memorizing it as he munches. And when that one is gone, there is another ballad on another box. If these are done by a good artist in watercolor or woodcut, the result would be quite welcome on any tablecloth. And that, after all, is the thing for which your ad men are working. Then, in this case especially, there is a chance for much free publicity for do not think that magazines such as LIFE would fail to pick up such an interesting angle on merchandising.

Then, for those who might wish to vary the routine, they could see a classical series. You could run a series of famous dramatic paintings on your box with a very, very short description of the picture. The paintings of American history now on display in Washington furnish endless material and, further, mama might like Willie to know his history better and papa really should review it a trifle through such a very pleasant medium. School teachers would be very glad of such a source. And those paintings are not exactly eyesores.

There could follow a dramatization of inventions done rather in illustration style than in the comic strip harshness usually used on such things. The point throughout is to produce on a box a harmonious blend which would place the cereal on the table instead of in bowls before it went to the table. At the bottom, on a colored strip, the cereal's name could be displayed.

There is little use to enumerate the number of things which could be essayed, all achieving the same effect.

Not to be discounted is the psychological effect on the consumer. Digestive and mental functions are closely interlocked. Corn Flakes could, in no better way, become synonymous for bravery and gallantry. Anything blatantly approached sooner or later deadens itself by its very commotion. But this is no obvious attempt.

If the function of packaging is to sell more merchandise and to place the merchandise itself upon a higher level, then the double printing of wrapper and box would wipe out its added cost ten times over by the good will created. And such a package, I trust, could be protected by process of patent or copyright.

Wishing you success in the New Year, I am

Sincerely,
L. Ron Hubbard

CHAPTER FOUR

The RUSSELL HAYS LETTERS

The Russell Hays Letters

A MONG OTHER GREAT FRIENDSHIPS BORN FROM THESE years was the two-decade bond between LRH and fellow author Russell Hays. Hays was a fascinating figure. In addition to the penning of highly authentic westerns, he held several key patents for helicopter rotary systems, coaxed fine skunk cabbage from Kansas dust and occasionally drilled for oil. Needless to say, and notwithstanding a penchant for chewing tobacco and the monosyllabic drawl, he also possessed an exceptionally keen wit. (Ron describes it as "the sticklike quality of a twig-bug, developed to trap the unwary.") Then, too, he harbored a fairly keen interest on questions relating to the human thought process—hence, the later Hays-Hubbard correspondence on Dianetics as provided in *Dianetics Letters & Journals.* As evidenced here, he had no less to say on the woof and warp of creative writing.

These letters tell us a lot. Hays has been discussing what he terms the literary "lift," or the plotting of stories according to an emotional curve. LRH responds with an equally elaborate theory on characterization as drawn from actual experience, e.g., "I threw away my dashing lieutenant and substituted a drunken top sergeant. I snatched up a Chinese missionary and wrote him as I knew him." They further have a few choice words on editorial restrictions and a natural aversion to the "main track" of convention—all while proving, as Arthur J. Burks so rightly declared, "No one but a writer can understand a writer's ailments." ∎

Below
Russell Hays

Left In Port Orchard, Washington, 1938

Cannondale, Conn.
June 30, 1935

Mr. Russell Hays
Wellsville, KANSAS

Dear Russ;

Your pistol received and contents razzed. So you're a farmer after all. I allus kind of thought you had some hoss thieves in your ancestry but I never did dream that you'd have anything like farming. Me, I'd rather dish roulette or chuck Chuckaluck or some honest gambling scheme. But farming—tish tish, Si, tch, tch.

I can see you in a mangy straw hat and a pair of baggy overalls, leaning on a two-barb wire fence chawin' on some straw kinda commentatin' on the weather, by gum. Your wrestling confined to cyows, and your perfume to manure. Think back to them good old days when all you had to pound was a mill and all you planted was rejected wordage. Yowsah.

Now all you dust off is a few storms.

Sorry I couldn't get at this sooner, but stories have been mounting on my desk. I've been trying to average five thousand a day first and final draft.

Been selling S&S lately, bless 'em. Soon, no doubt, I'll have a couple good markets under my belt—maybe slick. I keep trying.

Been selling a couple other names too, due to my unreasonable desire to bop editors in the optics.

Hope the ol' farm comes right through for you and trust God will reward you.

Best to your lady and ladette.

Checklessly,
Ron

March 7, 1937

Mr. Russell Hays
AERONAUTICS UNLIMITED
Wrastling Done Reasonably
Wellsville, Kansas

Dear Mr. Hays;

Your missile received and contents doubted. If I were diplomatic I would say that it took me all this time to probe the depths of your reasoning for proper answer. If I were cruel I would say that it took me all this time to read it. But I'm just busy as hell, that's all.

You froze, almost drowned maybe, and now you can't complain because Spring is at hand. I never saw any winter because I been wearing blinders while working, but I did write a lot of tropical tales to keep warm.

Your tunnel work should be well along by now if you've kept drilling at it and haven't let it drift. No kidding, how is the Heliplane?

Last time I dabbled in aeronautics I wrote up the Boeing plant for the Sportsman Pilot, used info for a short in ARGOSY, twice again for two other stories unreported. But as I spelled wrong the names of the Boeing President and the name of the chief engineer, I don't think I'll go back. Typical reporter, that's me.

I will send you a rattlesnake skin belt if I can catch any editors. An eighteen gallon hat and spurs would also go nice. I been thinking about getting me something like that as I also been thinking about getting a plow horse.

Columbia bought an old novel of mine, written in Encinitas. "Murder at Pirate Castle" to be a serial entitled THE SECRET OF TREASURE ISLAND. They paid me part and have written me saying they want my services please name my price and my price is about a dime a dozen so there won't be much hitch to it.

A novel I just finished in January is being published by Lee Furman Inc.—Macaulay Company. "Buckskin Brigades."

Same firm contracted with me in December to do one about Africa and gave me a plot. This is March and I won't get at it for thirty days, most likely and I already spent the advance. Whoa is me! The plot was awful! I'd like to retail it to you here but I feel too good.

One coming up in ARGOSY called a LESSON IN LIGHTNING. Be out the tenth. My Dangerous Profession series ran ten, I got tired, all finished now. Also had the lead this month in ALL WESTERN. That's make two westerns I've wrote.

This letter is not smooth, not convincing, lacks suspense, but the style is vigorous anyway. I been working up MURDER AT PIRATE CASTLE, total rewrite for ARGOSY as it is to be serialized in ARGOSY when it goes on the screen. This makes the second time and I'm kind of sick of it. I did 35,000 words since Saturday a week ago—eight days. But I didn't work today though I tried. Has to run sixty-five thousand, thirty yet to go.

By all means tell me the name of your friend in Hollywood so I can look up same and help him cuss you.

My, my, my what a lot of words not to say anything yet. Like those classic writers. If you take a half million words to a book, you're bound to make some wise-cracks in it someplace. Someday I'm going to drink absinthe and write a book like that so I'll be famous. I think I could write a million words without saying a thing in the whole million. Which lines me up with Scott, Dickens, and Fulton Oursler.

Time to go home so home I will go, dropping this epistol on the way.

I'd like to see you and call you a liar in a friendly kind of way on account of I ain't talked to nobody with sense since I left Noo Yawk.

Regards to you and Adele and Ba'ba' and the livestock,

Ron

Route One—Box 452
Port Orchard, Washington
December 4, 1937

Dear Russell;

It's been quite a while since I've zipped a letter your way and of course I wouldn't do it unless I had something to tell you about.

And so, with hopes for the health of your family and bank account, I plunge into the subject.

I have just found out something with which to repay that very kind favor of yours anent the "lift" angle on stories, and while I was working this out, I recalled something you said about your work before you slowed down and stopped key pounding. That you did stop has always been a source of puzzlement to me because you are an excellent technician.

This all sounds very serious, but it is serious because I recently found myself heading for the same impasse and after studying the situation out I came to a conclusion which is so ridiculous in its simplicity that it cannot help but be right. And my astonishment is not small that it has not been bannered before this. But I am not bannering it except to you, and as I respected your confidence in the "lift" analysis, respect mine in this.

If you take a squint at an ARGOSY which will be out shortly—I don't know just when and it may be out now—you'll find ORDERS IS ORDERS, 28,000 China, U.S.M.C. In it I adapted movie script writing to fiction writing, which is beside the main point as all my stuff is coming that way today.

But attend! I rolled one, 20,000, called THE CARGO OF COFFINS. It wasn't a very good technical job as I was monkeying with a situation I found in Casanova. It was a very unique piece of styling. But it was actually a second rater. But ARGOSY ate it without comment.

Attend! ORDERS IS ORDERS is definitely first-rate technically and has plenty of color and suspense.

ARGOSY says nothing about A CARGO OF COFFINS. But when they accepted ORDERS IS ORDERS, they commented to the effect that my Japanese were a shade too villainous, etc. etc., all comment on character as most of my comment has been.

A CARGO OF COFFINS was accepted with this comment, "I think you got a bit more character work on this one than in any of the others you have headed our way recently........"

This is all screwy because the characterization in the latter was definitely lousy. All stock stuff.

Now romps home a western, in which the editor says "...also the girl was a very unpleasant person and hardly worth the trouble the hero went to to marry her.......As

Left Remington Noiseless portable, a.k.a. "Super Seven."
This machine was continuously used through the 1930s
at Ron's writer's retreat in Port Orchard, Washington.

The Russell Hays Letters   101

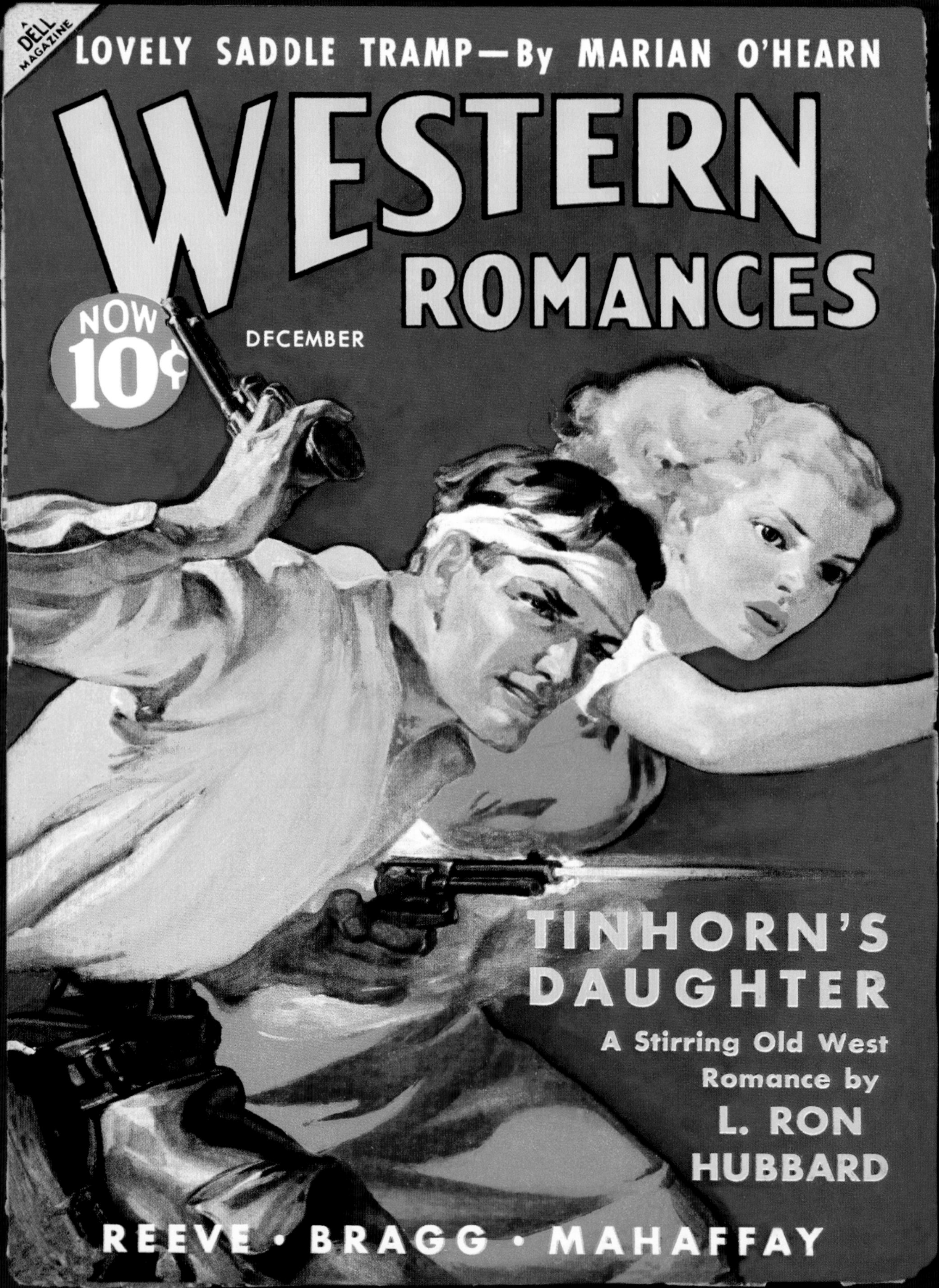

LOVELY SADDLE TRAMP—By MARIAN O'HEARN

WESTERN
ROMANCES

DECEMBER

NOW 10¢

TINHORN'S DAUGHTER

A Stirring Old West
Romance by
L. RON HUBBARD

REEVE · BRAGG · MAHAFFAY

you know I like my material a little more conventional than this, especially where the hero and heroine are concerned. That is, I like a heroine our readers can love and admire...."

That western was a pip, take my word for it. Technically it was all to the good. A swell twist to it, smooth writing and, believe it, good *characterization*.

Now that is the first intelligent comment I have read in four years, although it seemed infuriating at first. That western ed, Lawson, published terrible tripe, published a lot of my stories....see Tinhorn's Daughter Dec. WESTERN ROMANCES.

I have been gradually going nutty with such stuff. A lousy job would sell, a good job would come back. My best bits of characterization have been slammed home at me. But each time an editor said "characterization" both me and I thought he meant Characterization. And so, distractedly I would improve my *methods* of characterization and wearily return to the fray. My best plots came home, my best writing. It was enough to send me to the doggy depths and almost did.

I used to get by with pretty second rate stuff and now I've worked hard to improve my technique, characterization, everything. In the books for which I write I find bad technique, punk characterization. There must be some answer.

So, having explained all this dilemma, and after walking in circles for the last week, I've got an answer which has to be right.

My *methods* of characterization have never been under fire. The poor dumb editors have bitterly assailed them without realizing that they were shooting at the wrong target. They ought to be drowned for a bunch of blundering dopes, but they did succeed in teaching me *methods* of characterization by yelling about them all the time. I've got the ways and means of characterization too thoroughly catalogued for my own satisfaction that they can't be wrong. That sounds pretty broad, but a man can't help but make progress when he hammers on one subject for years.

These editors were trying to tell me with astonishing blundering that my *characters* were wrong for their books. Like you, I hated the main track and strove for unusual characters. And the more they yelled, the more unusual my characters became. You went off when you started to glorify your bad men. Remember? You did a fine technical job of that, but the fundamental fact was that a glorified bad man wasn't editorially digestible. And so I arrived at a "law."

Attend! Never write about a character type you cannot find in the magazine for which the story is intended.

Never write about an unusual character.

Experiment with plot, technique, characterization methods, but limit your character exploration to improving those characters which have already appeared.

Left Tinhorn's Daughter: Ron's unconventional western disguised as a conventional romance

I am going through my pulps with great thoroughness, cataloguing every character type appearing therein. You will discover that they are very limited. In a western, the villain is thus and so. The heroine is either thus or thus. The hero is emphatically such and so.

This, as I said, is too, too simple to be mentioned. Certainly everybody knows that. But do they?

Is it because writers are generally slow to improve their work? Is it because they usually want the most money for the least work? Is it because they have neither the pride nor ambition necessary to develop to any great extent as a general class? They started in doing something they called "slanting." Certain stories clicked so they kept writing them. They duplicated not only their character types but their plots. The latter was wholly unnecessary, unrequired.

That groundwork cannot be undone.

Lately I applied Newton's three laws to the mass of people, because I'm up here without anybody to talk to and pretty bored generally. The result is useful.

People as a mass obey all the laws of physics. Especially Newton.

Gravitation: They herd into tribes and cities.

Interaction: They tend to oppose any force acting against them as a mass.

Inertia: They tend to remain at rest until that state is overcome by a gigantic force sufficient to start them rolling in a given direction. They tend to keep moving in a straight line as a mass, mentally, and the force of gray matter sufficient to swerve all that composite thought is enormous.

Thus, you have the reason for the fact that every innovator is usually crushed when he tries to oppose the inertia of a people. Witness Paine, Erasmus, Spinoza et al.

Then, who the hell am I to set myself up for a suicidal piece of stream-bucking?

The inertia, moving, of the reading public is a mighty nasty thing to monkey with. Generations of writers have been busily educating this mass to recognize certain character types as being actual types. The mass is led to expect certain things of these characters and will not accept them if those qualifications are not present, or if other bewildering innovations have been added.

As one man I cannot hope to educate the entire mass of people into appreciating smooth technique of character development. I can only give them what they have been having. I can improve that with method and they're none the wiser. They only feel themselves moved or excited.

Do editors know this? Or do they just keep printing the same characters over and over because experience had made them feel—without making them think—that such and such a character has always gone over great and will therefore continue to do so.

Look over ARGOSY. You'll find the most horrible blunders made by writers in the field of character development. But their characters are a pattern. And despite plot, technique or lack of it, grammar, dialogue....in spite of everything, as long as the tempo is right and the story possible and probable, and as long as that character is a pattern character, the yarn will sell. Any number of technical sins are weekly committed by men who should know better and they get by.

All this, says Russell, is pretty obvious stuff. But it took me a long time to figure it out and the conclusion is pretty startling.

No matter what you do in a story, if your characters are pattern characters you can get by beautifully. If you have a gift for fictioneering, attention to character pattern will solve all.

I was going nutty before I thought this up. I recalled with misgivings that a technician like yourself finally stopped. And then I remembered that remark you made about your bad men. And in that and in it alone lies a volume.

I've been hitting the study end of this business pretty hard for a long time and I couldn't conceive the possibility that while I did a polished job on a character he was rejected because of "characterization." Well, I've got the last laugh but you're the only guy I'm telling. I know now that I can have all the fun I want in twisting plots and trying out stunts of technique as long as I use standard characters. Maybe I ought to be kind of bitter about it, maybe I am, but I'm going to put all my energy into making these character types even better by application of method to a recognized hero, heroine, villain or otherwise.

Incidentally, the tip-off to all this for me was that comment about "your Japanese were too 'villainous.'" My Japanese weren't the polite, hissing, bowing, apologetic gents fiction leads us to believe. Unhappily, I knew too many of them in Tsingtao and a military Japanese is a tough customer.

Added tip-off is my utter inability to sell a story which has any connection with my own background. I do it as it is, not as the reading public has been educated to believe that it is. So be it. Reality seems to be a very detested quantity.

Anyway, there it is in solemn array.

Blow the dust off your portable and tell me that everything I've written is pretty obvious so I can write back and tell you ¢%&W¢@&%!

Regards,
Ron

ARGOSY

10¢

COMPLETE
SHORT NOVEL   L. Ron Hubba

ARGOSY

DEC. 18   WEEKL

GUNS,

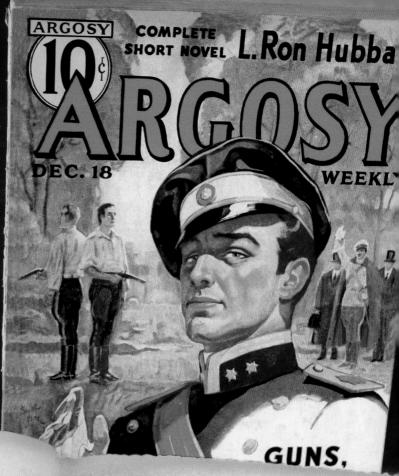

GOLDY

Orders Is Orders

By L. RON HUBBARD
Author of "A Cargo of Coffins," "Nine Lives," etc.

A
Complete
Short Novel

I

THE doomed city of Shun-kien poured flame-torn billows of smoke skyward to hide the sun. Mile after square mile spread the smoldering expanse of crumbling walls and corpse-littered streets.

And still from the Peiping area came the bombers of the Rising Sun to further wreck what was already ruined. Compact squadrons scudding through the pall of greasy smoke turned, dived, zoomed, leaving black mushrooms swiftly growing behind their racing shadows.

Along a high bluff to the north of town, a line of artillery emplacements belched flame and thunder and mustard-colored men ministered to their plunging guns.

Japan was pounding wreckage into ashes, wiping out a city which had thrived since the time of Jenghiz Khan, obliterating a railhead to prevent further concentration of Chinese legions.

Down amid the erupting shambles,

three regiments of Chinese troops held on, bellies to dust behind barricades of paving stones, sandbags and barbed wire, shoulders wedged into the embrasures of the cracking walls, intent brown eyes to anti-aircraft sights in the uprooted railway station.

They fought because they could not retreat. Two hundred miles and two Japanese Army Corps stood between them and the sea. Somewhere out in the once-fertile plains two Chinese armies groped for the enemy. But the battle lines were everywhere, running parallel to nothing, a huge labyrinth of war engines and marching legions.

There was no hope for Shun-kien. Once proud signs protruded from the rubble which overlaid the gutters. The thoroughfares were dotted with the unburied dead, men and women and children. Thicker were these ragged bundles near the south gate where lines of refugees had striven to leave the town, only to be blasted down at the very exit.

The cannonading was a deafening monotone. The smoke and dust drifted and en-

twined. Walls wearily slid outward, slowly at first, then faster to crash with a roar, making an echo to the thunder of artillery along the ridge.

War was here, with Famine on the right and Death upon the left and Pestilence riding rear-guard to make the sweep complete.

In the center of the city, close by a boulevard now gutted with shell-holes and clogged with wrecked trolleys and automobiles and inert bodies, stood the United States Consulate.

The gates were tightly closed and the walls were still intact and high above, on a tall flagstaff, buffeted by the concussion of shells, the American flag stood brightly out against the darkness of the smoke.

The building was small and the corridors were jammed with the hundred and sixteen

Americans who had taken refuge th Without baggage, glad enough to be alive, they sat in groups and nursed cigarettes and grinned and cracked and made bets on their chances of missed by all the shells which came s ing down into the town.

It was hard to talk above the cea roar, but they talked. Talked of Hol and Sioux City and Denver and a the superior merits of their towns. T their all was invested in and about kien, though most of them had not home for years, Frisco and Chi an Big Town furnished the whole of the versation.

A baby was crying and its whit mother tried t above the cata sound which against the wa side. A ma salesman tore h

The bearer of the message to Garcia had nothing on these two Marines battling across war-torn China

Rt. 1 Bx. 452, Port Orchard
Dec. 31, 1937

Dear Russell;

I am deeply insulted on so many counts that you do well to be in Kansas, me being such an excellent sharpshooter.

To begin, got a beautiful Xmas card from you all, for which I truly thank you and your lady, which you evidently didn't see sent.

"Orders is Orders" was not quite a jell and you sensed it. I had a somewhat ordinary plot to begin and suddenly in a flash of revolt I tossed out my lovely heroine and made her a fan dancer out of anger for all lovely and impossible heroines. I threw away my dashing lieutenant and substituted a drunken top sergeant. I snatched up a Chinese missionary and wrote him as I knew him. I back-slapped the Japanese for stopping me and almost jailing me once in Tsingtao. From a height of ideal formula, unable to control the impulse, I dragged the story into muck. And even then I checked that impulse. The result was, of course, mediocrity.

The best Chinese story I ever wrote was written for my own amusement. It is the tale of a second officer in Tsingtao harbor, a crooked engineer and a White Russian prostitute. The scene was a brothel. I was able to report accurately, had a point to drive, had a fill of laughing at the phrase "The pathway to sin is hard to desert."

The definition of art—if any definition actually exists—must certainly contain the phrase, "The artist's conception of…."

You have it neatly when you say that these characters do not exist. You drive home your point obliquely, as a reversal of your statements serves as proof for mine.

Go to a boy scout meeting, says you, and test tube your work. In itself, that is an excellent idea.

I have noticed a strange thing about my own operations. A kindly old fellow lent me a Plot Genie once. I was having a bad time building stories to fit the print. I plotted about three infallibles from that Genie and tried to write one. I was so sour and dead when I rose from that mill that I hated myself for days and days.

Left "Famine on the right and Death upon the left and Pestilence riding rear-guard to make the sweep complete." *Orders Is Orders,* December 1937

The Russell Hays Letters   107

If anyone begins to analyze foolproof editorial formulas for me, I also feel nerveless and sagging. Yours happen to be an exception to this as yours always have been clearly conceived and extremely interesting for their originality and I take a deep interest in them for the same reason that you do—mental phenomena.

Your "lift" idea netted me a couple dozens of acceptances.

But, in general, I have only to pick up the A & J, to accidentally read a half-conclusioned writer's mental miscarriage on the subject of commercial writing and something within me turns up its toes and leaves me like London's "vacant shrine."

Having sensed this long ago, I strove to solve what appeared to be an interesting piece of brain reaction.

After weary wading in darkness, I think I have the clear answer.

Even as you, I am a chronic individualist, which trait grows acute and painful whenever the source of my pay is run over into a category of mere mechanical application. I can't work like that. Neither can you.

You and I, to be serious, hold that certain things are true in this world. You have your conception of how people look and act, so have I. We both battle against any conventional tendency. We sullenly regard anything which tends to type anything about us.

The shock of having the last brick pulled from my granary foundation came with these steady criticisms of character. I did not like those characters as they were revolt characters, a will to refuse compliance to an editor, a stubbornness to cling to my own interpretation of life. Hollywood made the tower lean, Argosy caused it to topple.

At this writing I have here orders for at least six yarns aggregating about seventy-five thousand words or fifteen hundred dollars. By application of your analysis I could fill those orders swiftly.

Macmillan wants a novel and I have said that I would write it. To begin I am going over to the scene of that novel, Grand Coulee Dam, and loaf for two whole weeks.

And then I am going to begin a story which has been growing bigger and bigger with me day by day. There are no tabus save those against boring. And in the spirit of revolt I can guarantee the quality of that novel. I'll write it long and write it hard and if it is the last time I ever touch finger to key, I am going to pick up Grand Coulee, swing it around and slam it into print with such violence that it can't help but make a big noise. Macmillan's hallmark plus what has accumulated within me for five years, plus a habit of swift writing should make a combination good enough to haul me out of this 'mire.

I speak bitterly, without any humor, without any relieving lightness. But I am Rip, awake to the fact that I have been in the half-death of sleep for five years.

Know that I have enjoyed myself only twice in that span because I was able to embattle my wits without fear of sullen silence or lack of understanding. Encinitas, for a while, and then New York for a very short time.

Last week I remembered flinging myself out of my bunk at the age of eighteen, dressing while it was demanded of me why I refused to return to school. And I answered, aghast, "There isn't any time! I've got so much to do, so little time to do it...."

Yes. And that same spirit has vanished. But not so far into the yesterdays that I can fail to recover its meaning and the sensation of having it. Not so far that I fail to understand the method of getting it.

Certainly not sitting here on a hill top pounding out my brains at two cents a word. I have learned enough of my trade, have developed a certain technique. But curbed by editorial fear of reality and hindered by my own revolt I have never dared loose the pent flame, so far only releasing the smoke.

I *know* what I can put into my book. Plot and lead characters at hand, research remaining on the spot where the writing will be done. Strangely enough, now that I am working only to please myself I automatically evolve some of the factors which I have refused to accept upon command. My hero is going to scrap his way straight up the ladder in spite of hell and the course of his going will make dramatic—not melodramatic—telling.

I am sick of pulling my one-two, my verbal right, my energy left. And when I finish that story, the paper is going to be charred by the blast of its composition.

The novel field is so clear one pities the stumbling novelists for not availing themselves of the latitude which they are allowed. Certainly Romeo Reverse by Scurvy Gallon was bought only because no better yarns were being written. And, at the risk of great conceit unless you have read that gentleman, Wilder, Madam Mitchell et al., if a writer trained in the impact of syllables and on the rampage could not blow them all down with one hot breath, I err and know nothing of my art.

And here again we have analysis, but of a kindlier kind. Verbose, pseudo-intellectualism has been badly handled by all the above. Macmillan is panting for a best seller. The task is simple, the field gaping. I am mad enough to write it.

It does a man good to get really disgusted. Convention brands it variously: bitter and sour grapes. But five years ago I was a sky-rocket for enthusiasm and now I discover that somebody has been holding my hand to keep me from lighting the fuse. I'm convinced that I must return to that go-to-hell, "Anywhere but Here" existence. I started traveling when I was three weeks old. I lone-wolfed it through my teens. I managed to poke into live volcanoes and icebergs and Ladrone burying grounds and Peking hock shops.

Pulling punches is not healthy. Biding by the chain when the chain scrapes sores is the mark of the fool, the ignoble man, the groveler in the dust before the idols of the mass. And I've been pulling punches and biding chains. For fear men would laugh I have not said what I have thought. For fear men would be offended, I have stifled opinions which sizzled in my throat. And I know I have cared too much for that which is worth too little.

It's late and tonight I am supposed to go to a party so I had better knock off some sleep. I sure wish there was a chance of blasting you out of the land where the sun never shines and back into the Never-Never Country.

Best regards,
Ron

Wellsville, Kansas
3/27/38

Misterfer Ron Hubbard
N.Y.C. N.Y. U.S.A.

Hullo there:

I am very sorry to state that I have nothing to ride, razz, or pensively contemplate about yourself, immediate fambly, labors, or fate. Whatever the setup in the city, it all sounds very mysterious. Now Ronny, my boy, are you sure you are associating with er—respectable peoples? You ain't havin' no truck with gangsters, be you?

Wal, pardner, I read that there story in this here WESTERN STORY magazine; and dang it it weren't all right. No sour notes. Seriously, I envy you your ability to bat out that smooth a yarn. Of the writers who bust into the pulps or slicks either, there is just about one in ten who ever reach the level of consistently flowing out smooth ones avoiding sour something or others. In a way, the knack is like Bing Crosby's singing. His is only another voice, and by operatic standards a rather lousy voice, but smooth and no jar to it. A pleasant comfortable sound, no straining, no screeching, and no interpreter to tell you what he is singing about. Mebbe I'm just lowbrow and don't know what singing is, but I notice a heap of cash customers agree with me.

Things down on the farm are much as usual, a thousand things more to do than one shiftless being like myself can hope to challenge. Never before in my life have I been so trapped. Economically and climatically, I realize that it is very silly for me to continue staying here. I think I can guess at the reason I continue doing so. As a child, batting about the country with my mother, this place here where three generations of my forebearers had lived and died, came to be a symbol of sorts to me. That peculiar thing which as a child I never had, a home.

It is the damned, most intangible thing I have ever bucked up agin. I am the only one of my generation left here. Even the fellows I played with here as a child have all drifted away. I have only lived here a small fraction of my life, I have not a single close friend here, and yet everybody in this end of the county knows me by my first name. What I may have been or wish to be, means absolutely nothing to them. I am a symbol of something or other very close to the soil. I am the Hays who lives in the big house out at Blackjack. I am the boss-man by that illogical, unjustified thing called inheritance. I have a nasty feeling that if I pull out from here I am letting somebody down.

Doggone, I am getting sleepy. Just can't take this night life. Incidentally, my red-haired friend when you return to home and fireside it isn't going to cost you any more to get routed through Kansas City, hence you can drop off and tell me any new and vulgar stories you may be collecting at this time.

I yam, sinceripatedly,
Russell

Route One—Box 452
Port Orchard, Wash.
October 20, 1938

Dear Russell;

Just why I am indicting this epistle to you I am not sure because I hadn't ought on account of copious copy which lies in wait behind the eyes to pounce forth into immortal print—or is that "immoral"?

I have been cursing myself for a bum—which is nothing new—due to my seeming inability to get anything written which will magnetize the lucre. In truth I am having far too pleasant a time rolling around here swamping out woods and fumbling the idea of amusing myself by building a log cabin. This is the lotus land and if one doesn't watch, he hears the clock strike eighty before he thinks he has left twenty.

I made a flying trip to Seattle yesterday to get some things and stuff and incidentally to have the yearly overhaul on the mill. This time I added a nice little stroke counter as a sort of protest against Street and Smith's late habit of being particular with their word counts—they annoy me. Now I can say "Cyclometer Counted—9,919,334 words." Little contometer on the back of the machine rolls up one count for every ten strokes including space strikes. A word averages five with space, so I am told. I'll have to check that.

Haven't seen Mein Herr Egtvedt since my return but have been planning to drop in on him. Yore old friend Eddie Allen is testing this new flying fortress. See his Satevepost article? Never seen one of these test pilots yet that didn't have to chuck his weight around in print.

By the way, it worried me for some time that I had no particularly original method of presentation for the book and last week I thunk one up. I kind of sighed when I did because I knew I would have to do it that way and it meant an awful lot of revamping on the stuff already done. However I have run out of excuses and so I think I may have to get to work on it most anytime. I was further annoyed by another bid on that Coulee Dam book, Lords of the Roaring River, and if I do that I suppose I'll really go whole dog and write a piece of Americana two hundred thousand words long at least.

Best regards,
Ron

CHAPTER FIVE

Letters from a
LITERARY SEASON
IN MANHATTAN

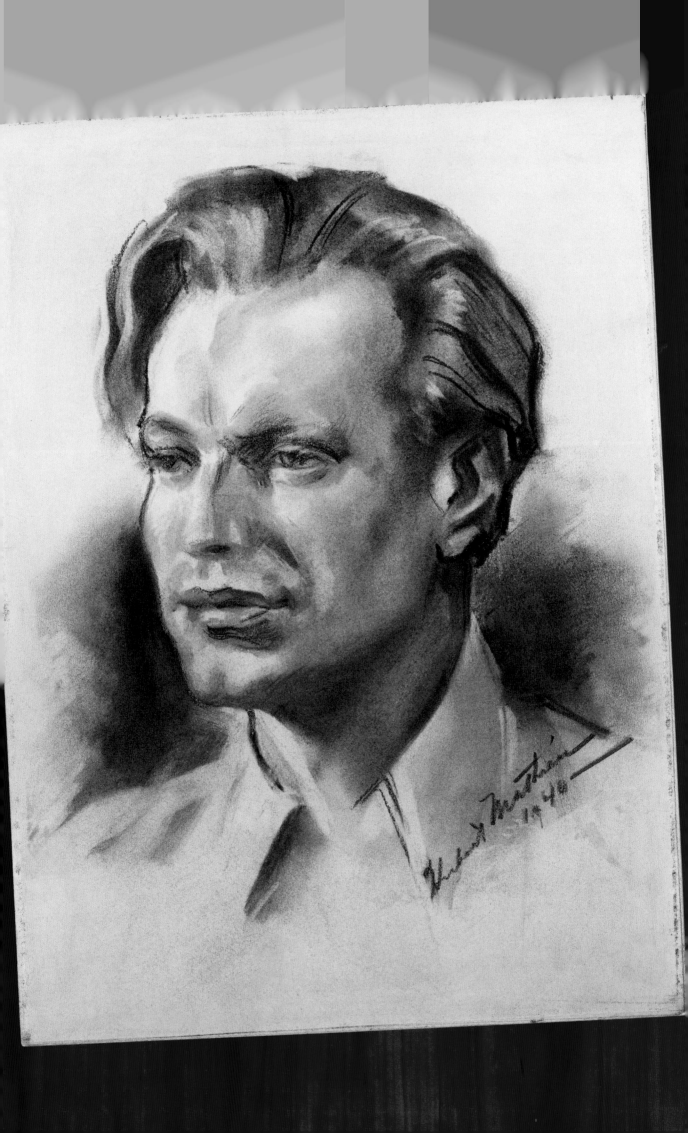

Letters from a
Literary Season
in Manhattan

B Y EARLY 1938, AND FIRMLY AT THE CENTER OF THE PULP fiction realm, Ron had established a semipermanent residence in New York City. In consequence, and quite in addition to the usual exchange with editors, we now come upon his letters to friends and family still residing in Washington and Montana.

Nothing so bespeaks the literary life as these letters from Manhattan: the elation mixed with drudgery, the inspiration broken by a dry spell, the occasional nod to the masters and the "write a yarn, disburse funds, think up a yarn, write a yarn.......Lord!" Lest the titles of works referenced here are not immediately familiar, those "yarns" still stand as among the most memorable in the whole of popular fiction. For having signed on with Street & Smith to infuse a mechanistic science fiction with a new and vibrant human element, these were the days of *Final Blackout, The Tramp* and *The Dangerous Dimension.* While in the pages of Street & Smith's *Unknown,* we find such pillars of modern fantasy as *Fear, The Ghoul* and *Death's Deputy.*

Additionally of interest here: we have elsewhere discussed how the bulk of LRH literary profits went to the exploration and research culminating in the 1950 release of *Dianetics: The Modern Science of Mental Health.* In point of fact: above the desk on which he pounded out his letters from this period hung a nautical chart of a British Columbian passage to Alaska where, in the autumn of 1940 and wholly funded from the stories referenced here, he conducted his famed ethnological research among north coast Indian tribes. ∎

Charcoal sketch by Hubert "Matty" Mathieu—*Saturday Evening Post* illustrator and "dear friend stamped with youth on the Left Bank of the Seine"

Hotel Knickerbocker

Sunday
July 24, 1938

Strangely enough, having grown extremely sour on the subject of writing—which must be worn off one way or another—I took a brush in hand. I am somewhat astounded to see what can be done with water color. Of all the mediums, Matt[*] said it was the one I should not tackle first so, of course, I tackled it. My draftsmanship isn't bad at all and my composition seems to be pretty good. It bears out my contention that medium doesn't matter when a guy is bound and determined to walk into the creative fields. The pity of it in this case is that I waited so darned long before I began to study such things. Of course this painting is a momentary release but just the same it is most exciting. I finally figured out what was this thing called the creative instinct. God probably creates energy. Man converts energy only. With energy God creates all manner of things. And because every form of life is somehow a duplication of the Self, then man begins to approach God's function when he sets out and creates wholly from the stuff of which dreams are made. In other words the approach to godliness does not lie behind the altar but in the province of creation itself. Hence man's excitement at creating anything from ditches to art.

Thus, we can follow out along that line of reasoning and arrive at some very interesting conclusions which indicate a great many apparently disharmonious elements in living.

I smear some paint on a sheet of paper. I put a soaring plane on the lip of a scud cloud and crack the lightning inside the cloud and light up the earth with greenish-yellow tones and label the picture "Excitement." Or I take a man and a horse and a woman and weave them together to construct activities in a world which is existing nowhere but in my own brain. Capturing my own dreams in words, paint or music and then seeing them live is the highest kind of excitement just so long as any of these things are wholly mine, untrammeled by other opinions and unchanged by other hands. A writer is furious "beyond all reason" to have an editor change a single word of his text. But now I think I know the reason. The editor has denied the writer the right to whole-hearted creation and ownership of a world of his own construction. A piece of art then ceases to become a piece of art the instant it ceases to be the product of one mind. Naturally nobody is nearly as interested in one of my stories as I am myself. Nobody will see anywhere near as much in a smear of my paint as I will myself. Therefore the critic is not only unwanted but is actually functioning something on the order of a grave robber.

I recall my jealous guardianship of my California vegetable garden. It actually pained me to have anyone touch it or to have to accept advice on it. I didn't really want admiration. The thing in itself was wholly sufficient.

And so it is with my pages. We must always better them the next time, always strive for perfection in them because if we achieve perfection then we have come as close to the activity of the Self as a mortal can get.

Ron

*Hubert Mathieu, *Saturday Evening Post* illustrator
who would later figure in Ron's essays on Art

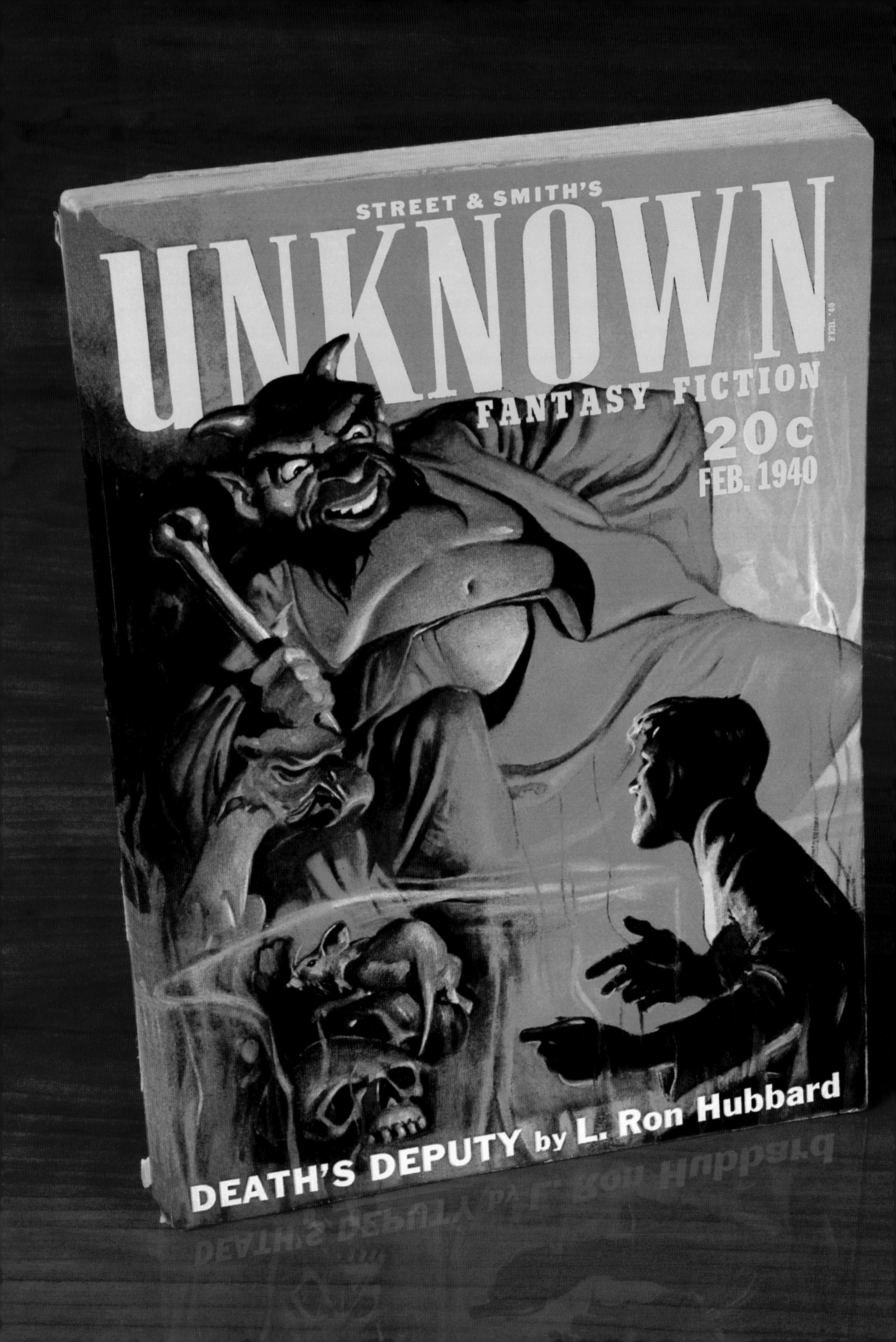
STREET & SMITH'S
UNKNOWN
FANTASY FICTION
20c
FEB. 1940
FEB. '40
DEATH'S DEPUTY by L. Ron Hubbard

HOTEL KNICKERBOCKER

Sept. 14, 1939

I am composing one for Johnny. He and I went into a huddle yesterday and out of it came a theme for a title, DEATH'S DEPUTY. He and I threshed around until we got the idea of a man who officiates, all unwillingly, for the god of destruction. Without volition on his part he causes accidents. No blame can actually be traced to him but he is always, in some small way, responsible. Incidentally, the elimination of such "accident prones" from large firms has appreciably diminished the accident toll. There are people, then, who seem to be magnets for destruction. Although rarely touched themselves, things happen all around them. One man in a trucking firm was on the scene of seven fatal accidents. As soon as he was removed from the firm the accidents ceased! And yet he had never been a direct or even indirect cause of those accidents so far as physical fact went. His helper, for instance, was in a truck body while this accident prone stood on the walk. A man fell from the twenty-eighth floor and killed the helper. At another time a motorist ran thirty feet off a road just to strike this accident prone's truck and kill himself—with no damage to the accident prone. Seven incidents like that, one after another and the jinx still follows. According to this, then, there is some basis for the maritime Jonah—and in the Navy there is a man who has survived every major sinking in the past twenty years! And was twice the sole survivor. There are, then, men to whom accidents occur, affecting those in their vicinity. And such is the story DEATH'S DEPUTY.

Ron

Left The immortal *Death's Deputy* as originally appearing in the February 1940 issue of *Unknown*

Hotel Knickerbocker

New York City
October 12, 1939

Yesterday I heard that John had bought my last and so I am starting today on BLACKOUT, a story of Europe after the war is done.

And so, beginning, I found that the typewriter wasn't working any too well. A mechanic had cleaned it a week or two ago and it hadn't worked right after that. So I made adjustments in tensions and now I feel like I am all thumbs on it. In fact I have never had it run quite so badly—which is encouraging when one is about to begin on a long one. However I suppose it will mainly be a matter of learning the new touch, and the old one was very, very bad.

I think I should probably do better to write this one in pencil and then copy it as I go along. That is a terrible lot of work but, somehow, I seem to get more kick out of writing that way. It does not take me very long to turn them out on the typewriter but neither, anymore, are they so very good.

Here it is almost supper time and I have not yet started my story. I must have worked on this mill for something like four hours and as yet I haven't gotten the touch right. But poor old Inky just had to be cleaned. I wish, when they go about fixing this mill, the mechanics would leave the tensions alone. But they never do.

I have supper with Matt during the first four evenings of the week. Then he takes off for Penna and appears again on Monday, having left Friday afternoon. In about ten days I am going down with him for a weekend, but I have to get out two stories first, each twenty thousand words. This BLACKOUT and then one for Florence.

The same old story, over and over. Write a yarn, disburse funds, think up a yarn, write a yarn.......Lord!

I think I'll get my shoes on (still a hillbilly) and go down to dinner. Matt ought to be around about now.

Ron

HOTEL KNICKERBOCKER

October 23, 1939

I am going on and on with this story BLACKOUT and it looks as though it may be a book between covers. It is already too long for John, though he doesn't know it, so I shall probably sell it to ARGOSY and then to a publisher.

Ron

HOTEL KNICKERBOCKER

Oct. 31, 1939 9:30 PM

I have just finished dinner, having finished my story not an hour and a half ago. I loafed along on the end of it, probably because I shall now have to do one for Florence about air-war over the North Sea. By God they better not call off this war and make a liar out of me! I have made my second story hinge on it.

An idea occurred to me the other eve for a fantastic short. Prof. Mudge comes back, in trouble again. And this time he is in *real* trouble for he had found how to control his looks and only needs a model to look just like it. So he walks into a phone booth as a man and, having seen a photo of a girl, comes out a woman. And then, when he isn't keeping tab on himself, glances at a cop and becomes a duplicate. And then when he uses Public Enemy Number One as an inadvertent model......

Ron

STREET & SMITH'S

UNKNOWN

JULY
1939
20c

**SLAVES
OF SLEEP**

by L. Ron Hubbard

SLAVES OF SLEEP

By L. RON HUBBARD

Author's Note: "A word—to the curious reader. There are many persons in these skeptical times who affect to deride everything connected with the occult sciences, or black art; who have no faith in the efficacy of conjurations, incantations, or divinations; and who stoutly contend that such things never had existence. To such determined unbelievers the testimony of the past ages is as nothing; they require the evidence of their own senses, and deny that such arts and practices have prevailed in days of yore simply because they meet with no instances of them in

HOTEL KNICKERBOCKER

January 2, 1940

I am all set to put the nose to emery once again. Johnny is short on shorts for both books so, as I am already Rene LaFayette on the Indigestible Triton, I shall also be, no doubt, Michael DeWolf and puhhaps Kurt von Rachen. Maybe I should shift that to Mikkel DeWolf or Mickale and thus run my pseudonyms on the foreign pattern.

So you are reading the classics, are you? Good going. I know you combed them all once but that was in the yesterday when you hadn't begun to think of stories as jig-saw puzzles but as entertainment. Magazine stories, especially the love stories in slick, are about as difficult in construction and presentation as tinker-toy men—built in two seconds without any change whatever except in the writer's mood. Love in the slick—or most any other thing in slick—is dependent wholly upon draping the simple frame gracefully. There is a type of feeling which is good but once seen it is always simple. Character delineation is too naive for a second glance in slick. Strangely I don't think I could do the stuff for it requires a certain mood which I don't seem to possess. A sort of lazy carelessness which irks me. And so when I see people getting a kick out of magazines I find it very uncomplimentary to their brain power for they become a "reader." Slick is cute and darling at times but never anything but superficial entertainment, mediocre on all sides. I believe tougher jobs have begun to crop up in fantasy than slick ever printed. And if you want something in plot structure, read SLAVES OF SLEEP. I don't dare monkey much with character because it always gets me into hot water. But I think TARANGPANG or McGlincy stand up rather well. You might, by the way, send me TARANGPANG with a couple extra sheets of the paper it was written upon. Maybe I can sell it now. But anyway, for character, Dickens' satire can't be topped. For tone and mood and objective attained, they don't come better than Poe. And for sheer structure out of incident alone Daudet and Zola are peers. For style Washington Irving is on the peak, for wit Shakespeare, for nonsense Carroll, for psychology Dostoyevsky. My ambitions do not go into any of these but I like to see what they could do with a given problem. Reading them for entertainment is nonsense unless one is entertained intellectually. Any gift of gab I have seems to be the ability to make a whole story run in moving scenes, dove-tailing character and action and working all things out in action terms. That is the goal of the action writer.

Left The enduring *Slaves of Sleep:* yet another L. Ron Hubbard classic from a famously prolific season in Manhattan

Of all the ghastly ghoulash ever gabbed, radio has the most choice. The Lone Ranger et al. are too idiotic to be given air space but America is doing its level worst to reduce any culture it might evolve by so bombarding the brains of the population with bunk that, before long, everyone will be numb to anything and everything. Senses can be so overloaded with messages that the brain no longer bothers to sort any of them and the process of thought becomes muddled by consequence. The overdose of blah on the radio will result, before long, in the standardization of ideas to the end of killing all ideas. Ingenuity is at a low and sorry ebb. There is something strangely soothing and satisfying about fairy tales and far lands but there is nothing but brutal degeneration in a radio serial. It does not stimulate the imagination but envelops the interest to the exclusion of imagination. It is canned thought. And veddy, veddy lousy thought it is. Those things aren't even well plotted and they have a tendency to throw logic out of gear. Leave radio to the mechanics that don't have to think and have nothing with which to think anyway. Its news and a little of its music are quite sufficient to justify its existence.

LRH

HOTEL KNICKERBOCKER

Jan. 18, 1940

I have been so upset about a story for the past few days that I have not written, not wanting to even touch this mill. However I finally got the plot of it licked and am doing research upon it.

The story will be named PHANTASMAGORIA and the theme is, "What happened to Dwight Brown on the day he cannot remember?" Twenty-four hours lost from a man's life. And if I handle it properly it will be something Dostoyevsky might have done. He strives to locate his deeds while missing everywhere but in the right place, for he fears to look there. He is surrounded, day by day, by more terror and apparitions as his solutions are gathered about him only to become hollow and half seen. He knows, deep down, that the day he recognizes his deeds of the day he cannot remember, on that day he shall die. And, having gone mad he has to choose between being mad forever and being dead. And if you don't think that one was a tough one at which to arrive and now plot by incident...! And John Campbell all the while drumming new suggestions at me and insisting I use them......! And five conflicting stories to be woven into one.....!!!!!!!

Ron

HOTEL KNICKERBOCKER

Jan. 28, 1940

I tried, today, to start PHANTASMAGORIA, having fully outlined it last night. But for some reason I could not think connectedly enough or establish a sufficient mood. It is a pretty dolorous story and so I suppose I had better tell it very calmly and factually, without striving to dwell on mood.

I've been trying to coax up a certain tone for the story. And I think a nice, delicate style is best suited. Paint everything in sweetness and light and then begin to dampen it, not with the style, but with the events themselves. In other words lead the reader in all unsuspecting and then dump the works on his head. Show very little true sympathy and do not at all try to make the facts worse than they are but rather make light of them. Oh hell! This is such a hard story! But I can see a sleepy college town with spring and elms and yawning students and a man just back from an ethnological expedition, called to take over from a professor who has become ill. A man suited to quiet solitude with a certain still idealism about him, who has come back to his home and his wife and is trying anxiously to fit into the picture which he so long ago left. If told almost dispassionately the thing ought to be good. In other words, I'll just write it. For I can't work up a gruesome mood. Ah, for a few days out of my adolescence! The character must take it all mildly, that's the easiest way. How I hate to make anyone "emote"!

Ron

Left Illustration by Edd Cartier for Ron's *Fear*

243 Riverside Drive[*]
New York City
Friday the 23rd of Feb. 1940

This place up here is a bit of all right. Sunlight and fresh air and the River and a chop suey joint that serves good chop suey up on Broadway and a bar restaurant on Columbus Avenue that serves three lamb chops for fifty cents with the trimmings. I won't be here into the time for hot weather for that is probably the only drawback this place has. But that isn't worrying me with snow all over the place.

I have a little cubicle fixed up in the corner as always. I got some monk's cloth—paid a total of three bucks for it—and a post of 2 × 2 and some curtain rods. By facing my desk out from the corner, I could then attach the five foot post to the back right-hand corner of my desk, the curtain rods to the post and so back to the wall and the place is quite nice for it dulls out all sound, even of the mill. Underfoot I have a Belgian rug about half an inch thick and just big enough to fill up this space. It gives the table here a little too much bounce but I can get used to that quickly enough.

Down at Street and Smith's day before yesterday I had quite a time for Wild West Weekly wants some stuff from me and, accordingly, I am today starting upon a short for them just to feel out the reaction. THE SHADOWS is the working title. Then Jack Burr and I are tearing through the old dime novel library in search of data on the early life on the Missouri and I'm going to do a 20,000 worder on the subject for him. He gave me the first of the original Jesse James series as printed by Street and Smith and there's quite a kick to the stuff at that. S&S has about six miles of shelves filled with the old dime novels and printed almost every one of any importance. They are nearly all collectors' items now and I could only get them by working with Jack. He had a terrible time trying to trace down the man who has the say about them and then all he could get was a promise of a catalogue. So today I suppose I should really go downtown and take a squint at that catalogue. However I have one to do for Florence before I can start and this short.

Ron

---

[*] *An apartment at same said address and thus a rather more permanent residence than the Knickerbocker.*

243 Riverside Drive
New York City
March 2, 1940

I am doing one now for Florence but it goes very slowly. I did a fantasy western this week, a novelette, but the pay won't be so good if it comes through at all. John wants "grim" stories these days like FEAR. He always wants again what I have just given him. I wish I had time to do REDHEAD FROM KAINTUCKY for Cosmo. Maybe I will have time. I don't know. Hell of it is, I know that the check for it would be all the money I would need for this entire period of work but still I am scared of using up time on it.

Made inquiry about Inky's turn-in the other day and discovered she was worth $30. She was running something awful but as soon as a salesman came up and began to run her down she picked right up and is now going great guns. Temperamental typewriter of a temperamental master.

Ron

March 10, 1940

My story is going very slowly. I was supposed to have had the thing finished by tonight but somehow I just couldn't do much writing over this weekend. Maybe the state of my hands had something to do with it. When I awoke Saturday morning they were a mass of bruises though they are almost wholly well now. You see, it's this way.

Fletcher Pratt, another from the circle of *Astounding* authors

Fletcher had a half house warming, cocktails at five. And I left the place at one A.M. along with most of the guests. The thing was definitely a success for nobody got really drunk and everybody had a very fine time. The hands come in because of Fletcher's purchases in Havana.[*] He brought back most of the instruments necessary to the construction of a rhumba band, complete with voodoo drums. Well, I must say that I never knew I could really drum before though I had tried drums a few times in the Indies. Hand playing a drum is quite different from stick-beating it. The amount of rhythm one can extract from a drum with the hands is remarkable. A fellow named Bill had a piano accordion and so he and I and a shifting group of others made the welkin ring. We had everyone doing rhumbas including the bartender. And John Clark says that when he came at six, there I was playing the two-hand drums (they are connected, you see) and when he left at midnight the last thing he saw was me playing the drums. Everyone wanted to know where I learned how to play voodoo drums so I was smart and kept my mouth shut. I am very definitely going to have a couple such drums sent up from Havana. All by themselves they can do very strange things to an audience. They can throb and moan and wail and roll and thunder and whisper like a parade of ghosts. But I paid with a pair of swollen hands. I did not drink much but I got awfully drunk on drum music.

Seems I can't hit the keys right even yet. I seem to have done things to my hands beyond bruising them.

Science fiction legend L. Sprague de Camp

[*] *In addition to author Fletcher Pratt's Havana Night, extraliterary affairs included the flying of experimental kites with Saturday Evening Post illustrator Hubert "Matty" Mathieu, BB gun tournaments with the likes of Norvell "The Spider" Page and ice-skating evenings at Rockefeller Center with any number of others from the hard-driven ranks of the pulp fiction team.*

I have a nice story to write soon as I finish this one. About a corpse that would like to be friendly. And then I have a couple more shorts to do in a hurry. And then maybe, if I can think of one, a novel, plus a 20,000 worder for Burr.

Played poker last night at Sprague's. The "Interstate Iniquity Association." I lost seventy-five cents so I guess I am still very lucky.

Ron

⬦⬦⬦⬦

March 19, 1940 (Weds.)

This afternoon David Vern, who has been sent to NY by Ziff-Davis in Chicago, called to ask for a short story in a hurry. I was supposed to be starting one for Florence again but I sidetracked it for a day and so am getting out THE CASTAWAY for South Sea Stories. He said he could not guarantee acceptance and it is only for a penny but fifty bucks is fifty bucks and I need the change of writing something like it. It's a pretty good yarn.

Ron

243 Riverside Drive

Gnu Yawk

March 21, 1940 2:40 PM

I should be starting another for Florence but instead finished THE CASTAWAY in the small hours.

THE IRON DUKE should be five thousand deep when I quit tonight, for it is due Monday and I want the check Saturday. Besides I have a stack of stuff to do for Johnny. Then S&S broke down and opened its files to me (almost the first time in history that they did that for anybody) and so I am being handed the Buffalo Bill series ten or twelve books at a time. It is much better stuff than the public generally supposes for Prentiss Ingraham actually was a scout with Buffalo Bill and ranged the whole West for the entire early part of his life. So there is material to burn there.

Ron

March 25, 1940

Everybody in New York seemed to be blue yesterday. Every phone call I got was deep indigo—Jack Burr, Willy Ley, John Campbell. And so I guess it was just a sweep of the town from leaden skies and drizzling, chilly rain.

I am now going to try to do a short called THE ALKAHEST. It is a very short story and may or may not go over but I want to warm up for a couple novelettes, one for Florence, one for Wild West Weekly, one for John and then maybe a novel for John. I am finding that I can't drill along as steadily as I thought I could and so now I have to put in several consecutive days work come what may in order to cancel out the last few days of staring into the fog.

By the end of the week I hope to have put twenty-five thousand over the mill.

Ron

243 Riverside Drive
New York City
March 25, 1940

Yesterday I had a little hard luck with Inky. The tape which carries back the carriage return broke right in the middle of THE IRON DUKE. No, it was Saturday afternoon, right after the IBM office closed. Anyway I sewed it up with needle and thread and it worked for a long time until I finally tried to adjust it. Then it broke in another place. I must have spent five or six hours over the weekend fixing that tape. Today, about one, a mechanic came up and put on a new tape and a few other things and now, of course, I have the dubious pleasure of trying to accustom myself to the new feel of the keyboard, with seven thousand words to do before I am finished tonight. However Inky got herself some new type in spots and the rest aligned and so the type probably looks much better EVEN IF SHE DOESN'T FEEL BETTER TO MY FINGERS. Damn it, it jumped to caps when I was fooling with it. And to top that, last night when I was making me something to eat I cut my finger, the right index, on a piece of paper so that I am very much aware of it. But the story has to be in and so I am skating along and to hell with it.

Tomorrow—or rather, this afternoon I am going down to research data for the KIDNAPPED CHARACTER or whatever the title may prove to be. I have to check history and so on at the Public Library.

Ron

The Iron Duke, as published
in *Five-Novels Monthly,* July 1940

Got the okay today on the Iron Duke. Florence was ill but dragged herself down to the office just to put it through, for she needed something for a cover. However, the front office would not allow her to use "anything foreign" so I don't get a cover again.

Tonight I am going to start to roll the Kilkenny Cats, second of a series of shorts. Then perhaps tomorrow I shall start upon THE ALKAHEST another short for the same market, though the first is under the old name of Kurt von Rachen.

Otherwise I am a bit bored. I have been reading Buffalo Bill and the stuff is pretty crude, so much so that it gives me a stale flavor. Ingraham is overrated in his knowledge of the West I know now for he never gives out any information and no description of the country. A rifle is "of the pattern used at that time." Etc. He avoids any specific data and is therefore rather useless in source.

This mill isn't running any too well again but I guess it will get heated up after a while. Feels sort of draggy to my fingers and persists in not striking or striking too much.

Ron

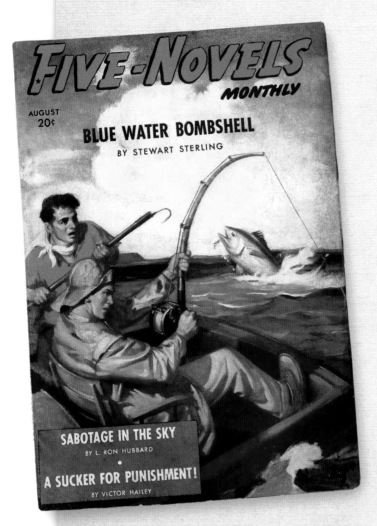

Sabotage in the Sky: still another white-knuckled thriller amidst astonishing space opera for *Five-Novels Monthly*

I am waiting for the maid to get out of here as well as Lavatory Sam, guardian of the can who always creeps in with her and surreptitiously swamps the bath. His real name is George but I can never see him without remembering a song about Lavatory Sam.

The radio is going with some sweet music. I am allergic to swing, particularly since I eat in bars with coin phonographs howling. The food is good and cheap but my nerves pay heavily. I cook breakfast and lunch and generally eat out. In a week or so I shall probably begin eating down at the Knickerbocker for dinner because Matty has been kicking and I'd just as soon. As a matter of fact I am lonesome and need a break in my day.

Just finished breakfast and it is three-thirty PM. I couldn't start that story and as it is due Monday I now have mill-fright at the amount of working I shall have to do in the next few days. The maid drops things. I just heard something crash.

Well, I paused while the maid finished up. And then I phoned Post and Campbell. The former and I went around and around about a rate. I want to do one in that direction. It's a plot which might run twenty thousand and John can't take it at more than eight thousand. John, further, has his heart set on something "grim" and I don't like to write them at that for they are very tiring and I don't think they are very good. Post says my rate is listed at 1¼¢ but sho I never got that from Argosy. He thinks it is wrong too. Anyway he says he'll pay 1½¢ if he likes the yarn. I want this market again for an outlet about Alaskan fishing stories.

I had better get going now on SABOTAGE IN THE SKY or whatever I'll call it. For time flyeth.

Ron

PS A static search party just located my mill and it is raising hell with the radios of refugees who are trying to find out how the war is going. I have changed a connection in the mill which is supposed to keep it from kicking back into the line but it is possible that I may have to go back to the Knickerbocker for I can't stay where I can't write and they tell me they'll turn off my juice! However I have the situation under control for today at least.

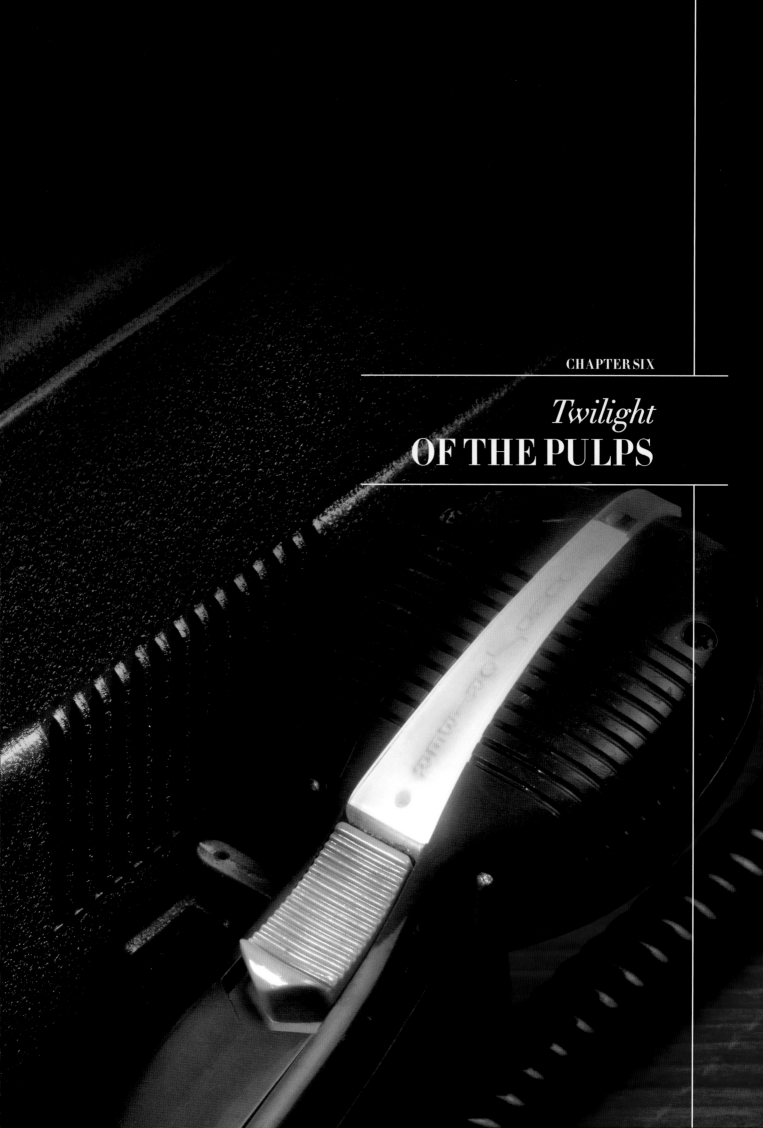

CHAPTER SIX

Twilight
OF THE PULPS

Twilight
of the Pulps

WITH THE ADVENT OF THE SECOND WORLD WAR AND RON'S commission in the United States Navy as skipper of antisubmarine corvettes, his literary life sadly ground to a halt. "I am even unwilling to write these days," he confessed in the winter of 1944. Then wistfully added, "but more and more I am beginning to be determined

about writing." What immediately followed from that determination were two historical romances, "written in bits" as a "practice run," and never entirely completed. By late December 1945, however, we find him rather more determinedly informing New York agent Lurton Blassingame, "I have begun a writing business once more."

It was a fairly heroic effort. For notwithstanding his claim to "normalcy," he still suffered grievously from wounds sustained in action. To wit: the muzzle flash of a deck gun had left him legally blind, while shrapnel fragments in hip and back had left him all but lame. In consequence, he could barely seat himself at a typewriter, could not focus on a printed page and, for that matter, could not discern the pages of his own books.

His immediate solution was the SoundScriber dictaphone and hired stenographer remarked upon in letters to the ever-loyal Leo Margulies of Standard Magazines. With the restoration of his health—pursuant, incidentally, to his application of early Dianetics—he continued to employ both dictaphone and typist in the interest of high-speed production. (Although even at his physical worst, he had still managed some thirty thousand words a month; while by 1947, he healthily resumed his prewar rate—an astonishing seventy thousand words at barely three days a week.)

As further evidenced in letters here, however, these were plainly transitional days, with *Unknown* by the boards, *Astounding* in hiatus and the pulps soon drowning in a wash

World Science Fiction Convention, Toronto, Canada, 1948; clockwise from far left back row: L. Ron Hubbard, John W. Campbell, Jr., Sam Moskowitz, Frank Belknap Long, Richard Wilson and Willy Ley

Above
On the road,
1948

of paperbacks—which explains the LRH requests for a Street & Smith release of rights for republication in hardback. Then, too, and even if letters to the likes of Campbell scarcely allude to the fact, Ron was soon to entirely devote himself to final steps of research towards Dianetics. Hence the references to his Commodore Deluxe trailer, "tricked up as a writing office," and otherwise the perfect vehicle with which to crisscross the country in search of test cases. Hence, too, the reference to his "writing schedule" as separate to an unmentioned research schedule. ■

Dear Lurton;

Forgive me for not writing sooner. But I have been in quite a spin trying to get squared around and in shape to go to work—and I mean go to work. Lurton, you are about to experience, come February or sooner, a flood of copy. You will have to hire squads of messengers just to get it around and an armored car just to pick up checks.

Wednesday next will be delivered two SoundScriber recorders and one transcriber and a thousand records. I shall call hither and yon and get me a typist. These new dictaphones are wonderful and even with the old ones I could roll out a volume.

I wired you a couple weeks ago that I would take on the 49 book if you had an advance and a decent contract. Maybe you didn't receive the wire, for I haven't heard from you. Anyway, I will, for with my setup I can chew one off fast, the research data being plentiful in this locale and in my files.

As you know, I roll enough copy in ordinary times so that sales operate as a sort of criticism service all its own. I know where I am going over well by sales. I very much need you for two vital purposes: to act as a bumper for rejects, to keep selling as only you can sell. This, I think, will answer its own question after we have been going for a while.

The part of your opinion which I value highly is that steering ability into markets. You and I know that this business of openings for certain stories is overvalued. Competition, to really good yarns, is never very serious. No writer who is serious about it and who writes well has much competition. You can tell me, from what you are receiving from me, what markets I should try next, in what lengths. I like to write long stuff. Short stories pave the road to the poorhouse. Serials are covers. With my present setup I can roll the long stuff easily.

I am going, at first, into a small circle of writing. Novelettes thrust in succession into several fields just to orient myself. I used to be in DFW, Black Mask, Western Story, air-war, adventure, sea, fantasy, etc. books. I may try again for those markets in rotation just to see where I come out best and get into swing. Then I want to go serial.

The SoundScriber dictaphone used by L. Ron Hubbard in the late 1940s to dictate some of his most memorable tales

Rog Terrill will buy. Jack Byrne, Jack Burr, John Campbell, etc. will buy if they get a special play on each story from you (for otherwise they will think I've turned my back on them, finding my stuff buried or unmentioned by phone). Then maybe we try some slick. Some serials.

Now, one thing, a promise requested before I close. I always wrote straight at my editors, seldom missed, habituated them to a lot of fanfare and showmanship about stories. When you start to get volume from me, please promise me you'll phone the editor for whom the ms is intended and tell him you are sending it over, making him understand it's especially for him. Otherwise my old boys, who've stood by these many years, are going to wonder what they did to make me mad at them, for the relationship in almost every instance is quite personal and deep. Please?

Best regards,
Ron

Box 270
Stroudsburg, Pa.
22 January 1947

Dear John;

    I had this one on the griddle and so finished it mid-novel to get something out. I have it on request but as I am going to write a limited number of science fiction stories this year, I see no reason to run a name which in this field is essentially ASTOUNDING into competition with you. The house requesting is a detective outlet for me primarily and I would just as soon keep it so. I get, by the way, good rates on why-do-they-have-to-do-its which is a shocking commentary on the bloody, vengeful mindedness of our citizens and precious public, who ought to content themselves with good clean opera. While I am writing otherwise, the house in question is struggling to get me out the list of tabus I ordered from them. By mid-February they will probably have whipped me up some fine plots! Remember?

    The novel is coming right along. The scientist will save the world yet!

Cheers.
Ron

September 5th, 1947

Mr. L. Ron Hubbard
Box 224
Port Orchard, Washington

Dear Ron:

I don't know when I've had more pleasure in a long time than in buying an L. Ron Hubbard manuscript. I'm only sorry it has taken us so long getting at 240,000 MILES STRAIGHT UP. Right after the manuscript reached the office I left on my vacation. I was gone a month, returning a couple of days ago.

Your darn good 10,000 worder will fit in nicely with THRILLING WONDER STORIES. I am sure the little boys and girls who know you and know your name will also welcome you to our pages.

Incidentally, we also publish, in the same field, STARTLING STORIES—and this magazine uses 40,000 word lead novels. Under separate cover I am sending you a couple of the last issues. Take a look at them and how about doing a 40,000 worder for us? Naturally in a story as long as this, we would rather see a synopsis from you first.

I am enclosing herewith a list of our many magazines and the requirements. The fields are always the same, aren't they—western, detective, sports, aviation, science fiction. We buy almost two million words a month here, and need a lot. Just give me an idea of the sort of thing you like to do best and I'll find a spot for you and tell you what lengths we need most.

Enclosed herewith you will find our check in payment for the yarn.

My very best to you.

Sincerely yours,
LEO MARGULIES

Box 224
Port Orchard, Wash.
September 8, 1947

Dear Leo;

Thank you for the check and the very pleasant letter. I have been sitting here in the darnedest rainstorm I've seen since Alaska and this was a beam of sunshine in an otherwise drab atmosphere. I am getting terribly bored with this climate now that winter approaches and think I had better load up my trailer and tow south. I have an aluminum job which is tricked up as a writing office—nice mahogany desk, book cases, patent chair, typewriter and dictaphone stands—and it sure saves me a lot of writing time. The rig has paid for itself a couple times, I think.

The place I had down in Southern Calif. has been sold through my usual lack of business acumen and I shall probably have a lot of trouble buying another, for they say real estate there has just begun to boom. But my aching bones are worth a lot to me, somehow, and so I shall have to put up with being robbed, for the sake of sunlight.

I'm doing a long novel in fits and starts for slick and have to have it done by December because of tying it in with the California centennial in '49. So I shall pause in the Mother Lode country a moment to check some data and then go on south.

Happen to notice you occasionally publish gold rush yarns in your various westerns. Might unreel one from all this excess data. I am not particularly happy about stacking up material and then not using it, but I don't know that you would be interested.

I note what you say about a 40,000 worder and as the length is an easy one, we might see what can be done. I looked over some Startlings I had here and will check over the two you are sending.

The story I have in mind is, so far, nameless, but it may please you.

This letter has been slightly delayed due to my preoccupation in starting on my trip.

I am enroute to California as I write.

A partial synopsis of BLACK TOWERS OF FEAR is enclosed. A fast report on it will aid my work schedule.

A possible writing schedule is also enclosed on which I would like your comment. This may or may not make sense with your inventory or desires but here it is. I like variety because it seems to keep me fresh in each field. I can schedule this because, with returning health, I can reestablish my wordage on its old basis.

I would very much value your opinion on the synopsis and the schedule and look forward to hearing from you.

My very best regards,
Ron

Nov. 20, 1947
Box 297
No. Hollywood, Calif.

Dear Forry;

I have just finished straightening up Death's Deputy. I have removed some anachronisms and changed some place names. It is very odd reading all this stuff written before Europe had been in the war more than a month. I am somewhat amazed at the little necessity for revision. This is no pat on the back for me but only a comment that all wars must be mostly the same.

I will send this to the publisher in a day or two. I have written also the dedication and the preface to Final Blackout but I have not yet had time to revise the story itself.

You may also tell the publisher that I will be delighted to sign the two hundred and fifty copies. I hope you keep me advised in the future on these other options and manuscripts as to when they will be required by the publishers.

I've got a stinging good preface for Final Blackout that ought to set the FBI on my trail, probably land me in jail, and doubtless help the sale of the book no end.

You may send a note to Bill Sloane if you want to to tell him that I will be very happy to do an extensive revision on The End Is Not Yet regarding dates, the outer frame (which Campbell made necessary), and several internal discrepancies.

Anent Fear: don't be afraid to send it to a big book outfit although I have my qualms about the shape it's in, for they don't like pulp. I don't know which of the big publishers is doing fantasy, maybe you have a way to look that up—although Fear is actually a psychological novel, not a fantasy. A good tag to the thing, to give it some face, might be to tell them that Dostoyevsky would have written it had he thought it up, since it is another book as reaching as Crime and Punishment, and is in about the same class. (This was a comment on Fear by a professor of English literature at Columbia. It is just about the nicest compliment I ever received.) Lord knows though that I could never write as well as our Russian friend.

I changed my mind about the house and have purchased another trailer for an office instead. I will be knocking around here for some time just the same. I is too darn cold elsewhere.

> Best regards,
> Ron

Forrest J. Ackerman, Los Angeles literary agent
specializing in science fiction and fantasy

Box 297
No. Hollywood, Calif.
December 28, 1947

John W. Campbell, Jr.
Street and Smith
122 E. 42nd St.
New York City 17, N.Y.

Dear John;

On the second of November I sent an Ole Doc story to you and to date I have had no correspondence concerning it. I am writing to you because I am concerned for fear my mail to you is going astray somehow. If the story is under consideration it is perfectly all right of course. I am just anxious to know whether or not it ever got there.

Also, sometime in November (I don't have the exact date) I sent you a letter asking for a formal release of the copyrights Street and Smith holds on my stories so that I may get them printed in book form. I have had no answer to this either.

Since the prolonged silence on these two (well over a month on both of them) I am just a leetle bit suspicious that my mail to you has not been going through with the efficiency which our Post Office customarily gives to documents entrusted to its loving care.

There is also the possibility that you do not have my address correctly.

If you just haven't gotten around to these things consider this letter just a hello. But, if there has been some slip up I would appreciate knowing about it.[*]

My very very best to you for the coming year, John,

Sincerely,
Ron

---

[*] *As LRH surmised, his third in the Ole Doc Methuselah series, Her Majesty's Aberration, had been briefly misplaced in the mail. The work eventually appeared, however, in the March 1948 issue of Astounding Science Fiction.*

Left Illustration by Edd Cartier for L. Ron Hubbard's
Ole Doc Methuselah, originally published in October 1947

Savannah, Ga.

Mar 8, 1949

Dear Bob—

Work stares me in the face and urgent letters have been stacked here for answer and so, with laudable industry, I take my pen in hand to chin-chin.

Markets were flooey in NY three–four mos ago and have just now broken open, looks like. But slick is particularly capricious even yet, advertising and such not being very flush, making the quill pen-blue-slip regiments rather noxious in their nervousness. Argosy ordered a re-write on a 10,000 worder (I'm the Great Dallas Strudemeyer there) and I re-wrote *exactly* what they said, adding not one word to their ms, just cutting several lines as ordered. Got the ms back couple days ago with the comment that they couldn't use it because the ending was suddenly improbable. Hadn't been touched. So we wasted 10,000 words of re-type. Sure sore. But that's the way the Ritz Boys act. Pulp was stagnant for a long while but now I've got several orders—Standard western & s/f.

Got a series at Standard—The Conquest of Space—in Startling. One an issue. Two other series going elsewhere but less steady. That damned Shasta Pub in Chi is trying to pay me percentage on their wholesale book price. Fantasy Pub, unless it swamps or something is the best book pay.

Some serious fiction is in the making around here.

With this cheerful thought, I leave Savannah the beautiful. If you sniffed quick when you opened this you smelled sunshine.

Red

Author and longtime LRH friend,
Robert Heinlein

1313 Cheyenne Blvd.
Colorado Springs, Colorado
26 March 1949

Dear Ron,

I wish you were around today. Ginny and another girl have been out panning for gold in the creek across the street from us. I patted them on the head, told them to have fun, and paid not much attention. Now they have come back with what they believe to be a nugget—and I don't know enough about it to tell real gold from pyrites. It *looks* like gold, but I can't be sure.

Long ago you were going to write down for me the so-many principles of the agent saboteur and the thus-many principles of the agent provocateur. You talked about them, but you never did. From a famous German work on Geopolitick and Realpolitick I believe. How about coming through on it?

I've seen some, maybe all, of your space-pioneering series. Two, I think. They are good—but my heart belongs to Old Doc Methuselah. I'll keep my eye open for Dallas Strudemeyer; I usually see Argosy since I sell them occasionally. Oh, yes! I hit a new market for me and the last in the world I would ever expect to hit. CALLING ALL GIRLS, a mag for bobby-soxers—with a short containing no fantasy and having a teenage girl as the central character. Now they want a series and I am a little bit dumbfounded. "Dod, oh Dod! What I do now?" I don't know anything about teenage girls; the story was a freak, a random idea which I wrote in an hour and a half, then tossed on the market.

Your warning about Shasta appears to have saved me from signing a trick contract. Thanks!

No real news at this end. I work away at the machine, with enough success to keep us eating but nothing startling. We skate, we read, we sleep, we chew the fat. The surroundings remain a constant joy but I am wondering seriously whether or not my lousy sinuses can stand the dry climate. Nevertheless I am happier than I have been in ten years.

Love and kisses,
Bob

Box 1796
Savannah, Ga.
March 31, 1949

Dear Bob;

Just wrote John W. a letter and gave him hell, the air-conditioned sort. I sent him an athletic sort of yarn and he bounced it—just a lousy old short. But his emphasis on the esoteric these days graveled me, since he doesn't know what the hell he's talking about. Which is what I told him. So to take the editor taste out of my mouth I am writing a love letter to thee.

Glad if I really was of service in any Shasta matter, not because I want to hurt them but because it might aid the profession a bit—which is all too full of pitfalls as 'tis. A greased pig is non-skid compared to those lads.

Fascinated with this CALLING ALL GIRLS business. My lord! But it's a good idea, though. Personally lately I have another tekneekew. (That's a French word meaning "methods employable in getting into things.") I completely apprehend your idea. You write a story. Then you get fan letters. Then maybe some of the fan letters are close to home. Then maybe....

Your request about the agents techniques recalls me that this here area is shore revolutionary, pard. They just ain't fergot nothin' about Reconstruction. Down at the library, all the way back in the vault, are four full length shelves of books such as THE PSYCHOLOGY OF REVOLUTION, ERRORS MADE BY ROBESPIERRE, THE POWER OF THE RABBLE, LAWS GOVERNING LEVEE EN MASSE, HOME BOMB MANUFACTURE, ASSASSINATION AS A POLITICAL TECHNIQUE, etc. etc. for about three hundred big, authoritative volumes. And I've never before seen a single one of them.

Robert, if I hadn't heard your last plan for Armageddon, I wouldn't even think twice about separating myself from this data. But what would you do with it? You'd go and put it in books. And then maybe the conservatives would pick it up and what would right wing people like myself do then? No spoofing, though, I'll dictate them off one of these days when I get this condemned southern girl up to a point where she can spell elementary English. I get a phone call every couple hours when she's working with a long list of words. Then she plays a record back over the phone so she can fill in the first draft. And loddie, she can really stretch a point, which is to say a syllable. Pretty, though. Awful pretty.

I'd sure like to help pan that gold. By golly, of all the things I do poorly I pan gold the least poorly. I can pan gold where they ain't no water, without a regular pan, without proper dirt and even without gold. Although I often find gold, that is the poorest part of it because then I have to stop looking and start working. So don't let Ginny find herself a gold mine. It would be entirely fatal on your typewriting. You got any idea of how much a shovelful of wet blue clay weighs? Don't find out. Just keep on telling her everything is pyrites but save it. Actually you can tell the two apart too easy to worry about. If it's yellow and you can dent it with your nail or knock a corner of it flat (an ounce of gold will thin out to a sheet an acre in extent) and if she flattens, she's gold. If she breaks, she's pyrites. Also get yourself a little nitric or hydrochloric acid. Put a little in a saucer, put in the article to be tested. If she stays there, even if she stays black, she's gold. In one or the other everything else under the stars dissolves. Gold dissolves only in aqua regia, a combination of those two acids. But once you see a piece of gold even if it's tiny, in a pan, you'll never make another mistake.

Boy, I'm sure not typing worth shucks. But that's because I'm just plain weary. Or maybe lazy.

Sure would like to hit the road, but I'm planning to have a little fun anyway.

The worst of this moving is shifting my working setup which is pretty exact. But there's a dog that howls all night out here and I haven't been able to catch him and give him any therapy. So I give up.

Consider yourself wrote to.

My *very* best to Ginny and my love to you both.

Ron

PS: Too tired to proof. You're a cryptographer anyway.

Dear Ron, I Realize That Dianetics Must Have Kept You Busy…

Beyond the spring of 1948, LRH correspondence with the publishing realm becomes virtually onesided. That is, while the likes of a Sam Merwin, Jr., at Standard Magazines still regularly called for L. Ron Hubbard fiction, Ron's typical reply was but a cursory note attached to a submitted manuscript. The reason for such brevity is not hard to figure. Although he still managed to meet editorial demands, the sheer intensity of research toward the founding of Dianetics gave him little time for editorial discussion. Hence Merwin's gentle nudge, "Let's hear from you soon," while Martin Greenberg so rightly surmised, "I realize that Dianetics must have kept you busy…"

Lest one miss the larger point, however, LRH output from this period never actually flagged for a moment. As a matter of fact, a chronology of published works between that spring of 1948 and the autumn of 1950 reveals some forty novelettes and short stories. Moreover, those forty titles include such fully memorable tales as the deeply moving To the Stars—among the most widely reprinted short works of science fiction in the whole of the genre—and Hoss Tamer, later inspiration for a teleplay of the same name and aired on NBC's Tales of Wells Fargo. ■

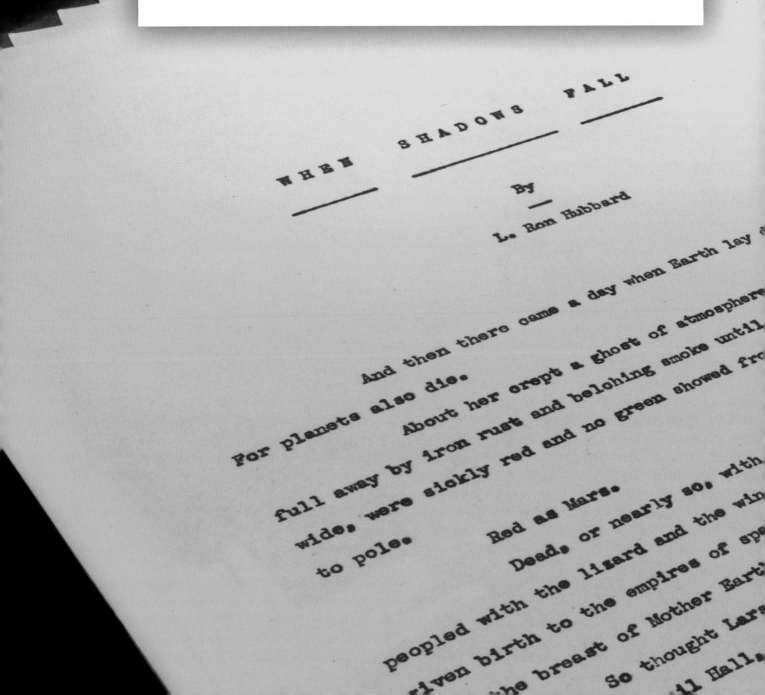

STANDARD MAGAZINES, Inc.
BETTER PUBLICATIONS, Inc.
10 EAST 40th ST., NEW YORK 16. N. Y.
Leo Margulies, Editorial Director

June 18, 1948

Mr. L. Ron Hubbard

Box 297

North Hollywood, California

Dear Ron:

How about some more stories from your gifted typewriter—either under the LaFayette by-line?

We need material at almost any length up to 20,000 words, since again we have enlarged the Science Fiction magazines.

Let's hear from you soon.

Sincerely,

Sam Merwin, Jr.

Science Fiction Editor

GNOME
PRESS

421 CLAREMONT PARKWAY • NEW YORK 57, N. Y.

SCIENCE FANTASY BOOK NEWS

August 15, 1950

My dear Ron:

As you will note by the date on the check I have been holding it for some time. I regret the delay but didn't know how to get in touch with you. Joe gave me your address and I mislaid it till now. So here is the check for the story I used in my anthology.

I have been waiting for a manuscript for Typewriter in the Sky. I realize that Dianetics must have kept you busy and no doubt still is. I have a lot of orders for the book and it was originally scheduled for this past spring. I delayed the book and it is scheduled for January publication and I need a manuscript.

If you have the time I would like you to give me a call. I will be at this number till next Monday any evening LUdlow 3-0965 or if you can give me a number where I can call you I will do so.

Cordially,

Martin Greenberg

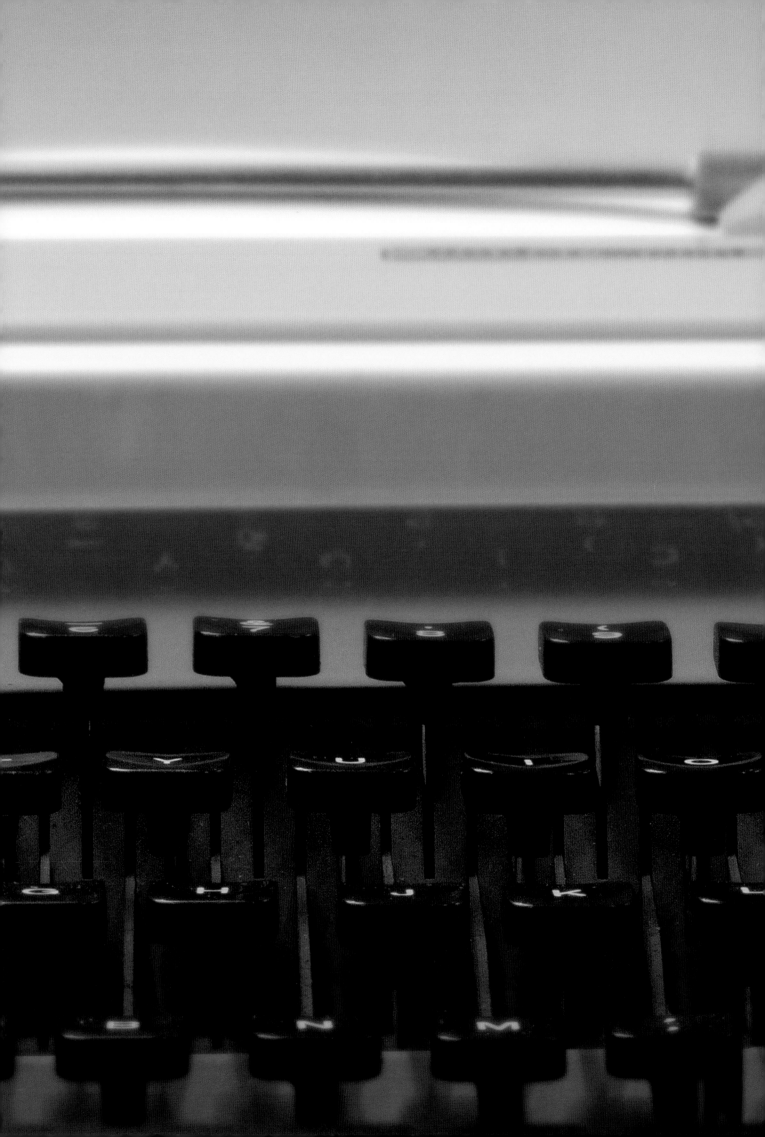

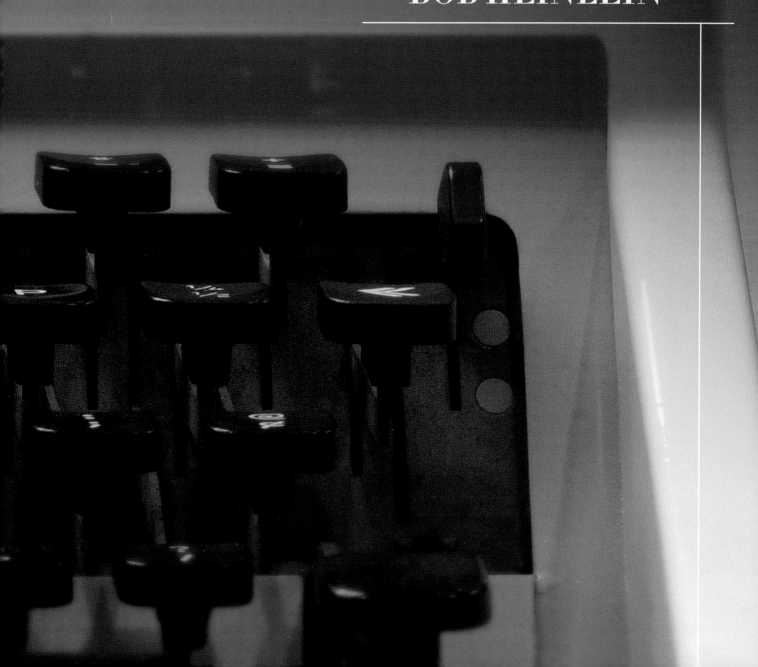

To and from
BOB HEINLEIN

Battlefield Earth
A SAGA OF THE YEAR 3000
L. Ron Hubbard
L. RON HUBBARD
AUTHOR OF THE GIANT BESTSELLER "BATTLEFIELD EARTH"
MISSION EARTH
VOLUME 1
THE INVADERS PLAN

To and from
Bob Heinlein

WITH L. RON HUBBARD'S RESUMPTION OF A LITERARY life in 1980 came what critics would legitimately describe as a master's return in genuinely grand style. The statement cannot be overstressed, for nary an author in the whole of modern literature has managed a feat equivalent to a *Battlefield Earth* and a *Mission Earth*. After a three-decade hiatus from the field came L. Ron Hubbard with the first works of science fiction to attract a truly mainstream readership in almost as many years—works with many millions in cumulative sales across dozens of languages and of such continuing relevance the word *classic* is the only appropriate term. That longtime friend and fellow giant Robert Heinlein had stood so firmly by is also fully appropriate; for to name a work of similar stature, one must return to his 1961 *Stranger in a Strange Land.* ∎

L. Ron Hubbard

26 October 80

Dear Bob;

Congratulations on your new book, "The Number of the Beast" published by Fawcett Columbine. I read it with considerable pleasure. The old master has lost none of his touch. Indeed, he has added to it!

It do look like us old codgers sitting around the stove at the general store, still have more git up and go than them young fellers.

I have just finished a novel myself. It hasn't been shipped out yet but it's all done! I had a couple of months idle and so I rolled up my cuffs and wrote "Man: The Endangered Species." That, at least, was the working title. It is 428,750 words long plus intro and is pure sf genre but in a modernized style and very fast-paced.

I said some nice things about you in the dedication and intro. I hope you do not mind and hope also that you can still blush! If such fills your modesty with horror, write back.

Anyway, it's a good thing for the field and fans we're still around. From other things on the stands, if tweren't for us, they wouldn't be readin' anything at all!

It is amusing that us should still be outliving and out-producing the young fellers. Do you suppose it's the fallout? Or maybe the water? Or is it because we're just too cussed to move over and let somebody else on the bridge?

More power to you, dear Bob.

Your friend,
Ron

15 Dec 80

Dear Ron,

Thanks for the very nice note and for three (!) Xmas cards. I want to be on the lookout for your new SF novel. Will you please let me know the published title, date of publication, and publisher as soon as you know it yourself?

It has been a bit over forty years since you published FINAL BLACKOUT—but the warnings in it are more timely than ever.

I hope this finds you and yours well and happy and no longer hassled by the busies.

All the best!
Bob

Robert Heinlein,
circa 1980

L. Ron Hubbard

Robert A. Heinlein
6000 Bonny Doon Rd.
Santa Cruz, CA 95060

24 December 1980

Dear Bob,

Very glad to hear from you. I hope you are getting yourself well "holiday'd" 'round about now.

You surely will be informed of the published title and all the details, as soon as I have them. I'll send along a copy, too, as soon as I have one to send.

Yes, over forty years since FINAL BLACKOUT. Now they're accusing us old-timers of being society's fortune tellers. I'm glad they've come to that, actually.

This year I celebrated 50 years at the old mill and so this is my commemoration piece to the occupation and my friends in it.

I hope you enjoy it and thanks for all your good wishes.

All the best to you too, Bob. I hope 1981 brings wonderful things to you and yours.

Love,
Ron

Robert A. Heinlein
6000 Bonny Doon Road
Santa Cruz County
California 95060

16 Dec 1982

Dear Ron,

BATTLEFIELD EARTH is a terrific story!

It puts me in mind of FINAL BLACKOUT in its flavor, but with this difference: It is a much more complex story with more characters drawn in full, a much longer story and one that, by being longer, has room enough for you to treat far more subjects in depth—serious subjects worthy of thorough treatment.

It was a good story from page one, then it got better when we reached Scotland, then still better in Africa, then again when ships from other cultures showed up, then (for my taste) reached its high point, and stayed there, when you revealed that the little gray men were intergalactic bankers.

The carefully underplayed comedy you made of this development I found delicious.

It's a great story, Ron. I hope it sells a million copies in hardback. It tickles me enormously to see you turn out such a masterpiece in your seventieth year—it makes these "new wave" writers who can't write English and don't know science (or much of anything else) look silly.

Again let me say how much I enjoyed BATTLEFIELD EARTH.

Always your friend,
Bob

Epilogue

In writing an adventure story
a writer has to know that he is adventuring
for a lot of people who cannot. The writer has to
take them here and there about the globe
and show them excitement and
love and realism.

L. RON HUBBARD

APPENDIX

GLOSSARY

A

A & J: an abbreviation for *Author & Journalist,* a writer trade magazine. Page 108.

absinthe: a green, bitter-tasting alcoholic drink. Page 99.

accordion, piano: also *accordion,* a portable wind instrument having a large bellows (a device for producing a strong current of air by expanding and contracting) that forces air through small metal reeds, a keyboard for the right hand and buttons for playing single notes with the left hand. Page 136.

adios: a Spanish word meaning goodbye. Page 18.

admixture: an element or substance added by mixing. Page 77.

advance: a sum of money paid before it is due. For example, a writer may receive money from a publisher, magazine, etc., for a story still in progress and not yet completed or as an advance against royalties while still awaiting publication. By *royalties* is meant an agreed portion of the income from a work, paid to its author, composer, etc., by a publisher, etc., usually a percentage of the price of each copy sold. Page 20.

Adventure: an American pulp magazine founded in 1910. One of the pulps produced by Popular Publications, the magazine featured adventure and fiction stories. Page 2.

aeronautics: the science, art, theory and practice of designing, building and operating aircraft. Page 98.

affairs: ordinary business or pursuits of life. Page 22.

agent provocateur: a person employed to associate himself with members of a group and, by pretended sympathy with their aims or attitudes, to incite them to some illegal or harmful action, making them liable to capture or arrest and punishment; secret agent or undercover man. Page 157.

agent saboteur: a person employed to engage in *sabotage,* the deliberate damaging or destroying of property or equipment to weaken an enemy or to make a protest. Page 157.

aggregating: amounting to (the number of). Page 108.

air-conditioned: used figuratively to mean made cooler; had some of the heat (as from anger) removed. Page 158.

air, up in the: not yet settled or decided; in suspense. Page 21.

Alaska: a state of the United States in northwestern North America, separated from the other mainland states by part of Canada. Page 119.

alfalfa: a tall plant often grown as animal food. Page 65.

alimony: an allowance paid to a person by that person's spouse or former spouse for maintenance, granted by a court upon a legal separation or a divorce. Page 9.

alkahest: the universal solvent sought by the *alchemists,* those practicing alchemy. In medieval times, *alchemy* was an unscientific form of chemistry that attempted to change metals such as lead into gold and to discover a substance that would cure all disease and prolong life. Page 138.

Allen, Eddie: Edmund T. "Eddie" Allen (1896–1943), American test pilot and engineer. From the mid-1920s he was involved in flight-testing some of the most famous aircraft of all time, including a number of the technologically advanced craft developed during World War II. Page 114.

alley, down the: on the mark; effective. From *alley,* the long, narrow, smooth expanse of floor down which a ball is rolled in bowling. Page 41.

All Frontiers Are Jealous: an LRH story first published in *Five-Novels Monthly* magazine in June 1937. An American engineer surveying the route of a railway in Africa saves a girl from a fierce native tribe, then takes on the tribal chief in a face-to-face encounter. (Prior to publication, the story had the title *Vanguard to Steel.*) Page 21.

all right, a bit of: very good or pleasant; more than acceptable. Page 134.

all thumbs: lacking physical coordination, skill or grace; clumsy or awkward, as if one's hands contained all thumbs and no fingers. Page 124.

allus: a spelling of *always* representing an informal or humorous pronunciation. Page 96.

Alpha Centauri: the third-brightest star in the sky, visible only to observers in the Southern Hemisphere. It is the nearest bright star to Earth. Page 45.

American Fiction Guild: a national organization of magazine fiction writers and novelists in the United States in the 1930s. L. Ron Hubbard was the president of the New York chapter in 1936. (A *guild* is an organization of persons with related interests, goals, etc., especially one formed for mutual aid or protection.) Page 61.

Americanism: something, such as a custom, trait or belief, that is characteristic of the United States of America or its citizens. Page 89.

American Mercury: a monthly American literary magazine founded in the early 1900s by journalist and editor H. L. Mencken (1880–1956). The magazine featured works by the most distinguished authors of the time, including short stories, plays and poems, as well as articles covering American politics, government, society, industry and science. Page 54.

amuck, running: becoming involved in wild and dangerous adventures. Page 11.

anachronism: something from a different period of time. For example, a modern idea or invention wrongly placed in a historical setting in fiction or drama. Page 152.

anent: in regard to; about; concerning. Page 101.

angle: the point of view from which something is written or said, especially when intended to interest a particular audience. Also, the action of writing something from such a point of view. Page 18.

anthology: a book or other collection of selected writings by various authors, usually in the same literary form or the same period or on the same subject. Page 55.

Anytown, USA: any real or fictional community regarded as a typical small town in the United States. Page 2.

apparition: a supernatural appearance of a person or thing; a ghost or phantom. Page 131.

apprehend: understand the importance, significance or meaning of something. Page 158.

aqua regia: a mixture of two powerful acids, one of the only substances that can dissolve gold, itself termed the "royal metal." *Royal* in this context refers to the ability of gold to react with just a very few substances; most of the time, it remains pure and therefore superior to other substances. *Aqua regia* is Latin, meaning "royal water." Page 159.

Arabian Nights: stories written on themes similar to those found in *The Arabian Nights* (also called *A Thousand and One Nights*), a collection of approximately two hundred Persian-Indian-Arabian tales of magic adventures, genies and love. Many of the stories, which date from the tenth century A.D., reflect the power and wealth of the ancient city of Baghdad, capital of present-day Iraq. Page 41.

Argosy: an American fiction magazine published by the Frank A. Munsey Company, first produced in the late 1800s. Containing science fiction, fantasy and other genres, *Argosy* featured some of the best adventure writers of the twentieth century. (The word *argosy* originally meant a large merchant ship and figuratively came to mean a rich, plentiful store or supply of something.) Page 7.

Armageddon: any "final" battle on a large scale that usually marks the doom of someone or something and that is so decisive that any renewed or further conflict is made impossible. *Armageddon* is the place (or the battle itself) in the Bible where the final battle between the forces of good and evil will take place. Page 158.

Around-the-World affair: a reference to a contest sponsored by three New York newspapers, each of which sent a reporter to travel around the world in commercial airlines. Starting on 30 September 1936, the reporters left the US and traveled across Europe and then Asia, across the Pacific and back to the US. Herbert Ekins of the *World-Telegram* won the competition after an eighteen-day journey. Dorothy Kilgallen, the twenty-three-year-old reporter for the *Evening Journal,* took second place with a round trip of twenty-one days, finishing just minutes ahead of reporter Leo Kieran of the *New York Times*. Page 18.

artisan: a skilled worker who makes things by hand. Page 65.

arty: having or showing artistic qualities in an insincere or superficial way. Page 63.

assaying: analyzing a substance by weighing, measuring, calculating, etc., to determine the amount or proportion of valuable metal contained in rock or soil. Page 15.

Astounding (Science Fiction): a pulp magazine founded in 1930 as *Astounding Stories of Super Science,* which featured adventure stories and, later, science fiction. In March 1933 *ASF* ceased publication. However, shortly after this the title was bought by Street & Smith Publishing, which restored it to its monthly schedule, changing the name to *Astounding Stories.* The magazine became a going concern and in 1937 Street & Smith appointed a young writer, John W. Campbell, Jr. (1910–1971), as its editor and changed its name to *Astounding Science Fiction.* Page 8.

attend: pay attention; listen and consider. Page 101.

avaricious: having or showing *avarice,* extreme greed for wealth or possessions. Page 30.

avocation: something a person does in addition to a principal occupation, especially for pleasure; a hobby. Page 54.

B

Ba'ba': a playful spelling of *baby.* Page 99.

backhanded slap: literally, a blow with the back of the hand. To *backhand* someone is to hit or strike him with the palm of the hand turned toward one's body and the back of the hand turned in the direction of the stroke or slap. Used here figuratively to refer to a malicious or harmful attack. Page 54.

back-slapped: literally, slapped (someone) back, here used figuratively to mean blocked or prevented (someone or something) from being viewed favorably. Page 107.

back (something): support (an activity, project or the like), as with authority, influence, help or money. Page 18.

Baffin Land: also *Baffin Island,* a Canadian island in the Arctic Ocean, between Greenland and northern Canada, approximately 1,000 miles (1,600 kilometers) long. Page 70.

ballad(s): a story in poetic form, often of folk origin and intended to be sung. Page 88.

ball, on the: a phrase indicating intelligence or ability. If someone is said to have stuff *on the ball,* he is considered to have competence, intelligence or ability. Page 66.

banana oil: insincere talk; nonsense. Page 53.

banana republic: a small country that is economically dependent on a single export commodity, such as bananas, and is typically governed by a dictator or the armed forces. Page 51.

bang-up: first-rate, excellent; the finest or best. Page 26.

bannered: given extreme importance. From a *banner headline,* a newspaper headline that extends across the top of a page, usually the front page. (A *banner* is literally a long strip of cloth with an advertisement, greeting, etc., lettered on it.) Page 101.

barb wire fence, two-: a fence made of a type of strong wire that has barbs fastened on it. A *barb* is a short piece of wire twisted around the main wire and having sharp points that stick out. On *two-barb wire,* each barb has two sharp points. Some types of barbed wire have barbs with four sharp points. Barbed wire is used to prevent people or animals from entering or leaving a place, especially a field. Page 96.

bargain, in the: in addition; besides. Page 31.

barnstorming: in the early days of aviation, touring (the country) giving short airplane rides, exhibitions of stunt flying, etc. This term comes from the use of barns as hangars. Page 15.

barren ground, fall on: be unproductive of results or gain; lack the intended effect. *Barren ground* is land that does not produce plants; bare ground. Page 85.

batting about: going or moving around in a casual or aimless way. Page 112.

BB gun: a low-powered gun that uses air pressure to shoot small metal balls, whose size (.18 inch or .46 centimeter in diameter) is designated as "BB." Page 136.

beachcomber: a person who wanders along beaches looking for useful or valuable things. Page 70.

beans, spill the: reveal secret information. Page 9.

bellhop: (also *bellboy*) a person employed, especially by a hotel or club, to run errands, carry luggage, etc. Page 2.

belligerent: showing a readiness to fight or quarrel; aggressively hostile. Page 42.

beneficence: the quality or state characterized by having kindly feelings (for someone). Page 34.

Benét, Stephen Vincent: (1898–1943) American poet and novelist. Benét's works are drawn largely from American history and folklore. Page 42.

beset: plagued or troubled. Page 32.

bespeaks: shows; indicates; is a sign of. Page 119.

biding: tolerating or enduring something. Page 110.

Big Five: the five publishing companies: Popular, Standard, Munsey, Dell, Street & Smith. Page 54.

Big Town, the: a nickname for New York City. Page 62.

Blackfeet: a Native North American people living in Montana, a state in the northwestern part of the United States. Page 30.

Blackfoot Nation: the group of Native North American peoples including the Blackfeet of Montana and several tribes now living in Canada. The Blackfoot Nation controlled areas that were fought over by fur traders in the 1800s. Page 30.

Blackjack: a town about 40 miles (64 kilometers) southwest of Kansas City, Kansas, a state in the western part of the central United States. Blackjack is a few miles northwest of Wellsville, Kansas. Page 112.

Black Mask: one of the best-known and admired pulp fiction magazines. Originally an all-around publication that included detective, westerns and aviation stories, *Black Mask* later focused on detective fiction, publishing stories by top writers in the field. Page 147.

blinders: something that permits a person to look at only one thing. From the two flaps on a horse's bridle that prevent sight of objects at his sides. Used humorously. Page 98.

blue clay: a type of clay often found in association with concentrations of valuable minerals, such as gold and silver. Page 159.

blue pencil: a pencil with blue lead used chiefly in marking changes or corrections and the like, as by an editor. Page 77.

boards, by the: be lost, neglected or destroyed. The term *boards* in nautical language refers to the side of a wooden sailing ship, and the phrase *by the board* originated in the days of sailing ships when in the height of a storm, a mast was broken and it was up to the skipper to either save it or let it go by the board—fall over the side of the ship to destruction. Page 145.

bobby-soxers: an informal term for teenage girls of the 1940s and 1950s. From *bobby socks* (or *sox*), ankle socks that fold over at the top, popular among teenage girls of this time period. Page 157.

Bodin, Ed: a literary agent, located in New York City, who represented L. Ron Hubbard during much of the 1930s. Page 2.

Boeing: a United States aircraft company founded in 1916 that became one of the world's largest manufacturers of military and commercial aircraft. Named after its founder, William E. Boeing (1881–1956). Page 98.

borne the brunt of: carried or sustained the heaviest or hardest part of something. From *borne,* carried, sustained, endured, and *brunt,* the heaviest or hardest part. Page 85.

bounce: throw something out as being inadequate for one's purpose. Page 45.

Boxers: members of a Chinese secret society whose name refers to the fighting (boxing) skills they practiced. They carried out an unsuccessful uprising, the Boxer Rebellion (1889–1900), aimed at removing all foreigners and foreign influence from China. In June 1900, over one hundred thousand Boxers occupied Beijing and besieged Westerners and Chinese Christians there. US Marines defended the besieged people and the rebellion was finally put down through the efforts of an international force of British, French, Russian, American, German and Japanese troops. Page 16.

box top: the top part of a box containing a commercial product, such as breakfast cereal, which usually includes the brand name of the product. Box tops are sometimes used as part of a promotional campaign to attract consumers with a free gift, offered in exchange for a specified number of box tops. To receive the advertised item, the consumer purchases the product, tears off the box top, which acts as proof of purchase, and sends it to the manufacturer. Page 90.

Bradbury, Ray: (1920–) award-winning American writer of science fiction, fantasy and other genres. Notable among his more than six hundred short stories, novels, poems, children's books and screenplays are *The Martian Chronicles* (1950), *Fahrenheit 451* (1953) and his screenplay for the 1956 film *Moby Dick*. Page 1.

brand: kind or type. Page 71.

bread and butter: one's livelihood; routine work as a source to provide an income. Page 63.

break, made a: broke away; escaped. Page 70.

Bremerton: a city in western Washington, a state in the northwest United States, on the Pacific coast. The large US Naval Yard in Bremerton was established in 1891 and provides maintenance for every class of naval vessel. Page 20.

brigade(s): in the Canadian and US fur trade, a convoy of canoes, sleds, wagons or pack animals used to supply trappers during the eighteenth and nineteenth centuries. Page 8.

British Columbian: of or having to do with British Columbia, a province in western Canada on the Pacific coast. Page 119.

broke: in a position of being without any money; penniless. Page 63.

broke down: ended any resistance to doing something; yielded. Page 138.

brooding: seeming to contain some silent threat or danger. Page 8.

Brown, John: (1800–1859) a radical antislavery campaigner who, in attempting to free slaves in the southern United States, staged an unsuccessful raid on the federal arsenal at Harpers Ferry, Virginia (now West Virginia). Brown and eighteen followers captured the arsenal but were forced to surrender. Brown was later convicted of treason and hung. *See also* **Harpers Ferry.** Page 16.

Bruce, George: (1898–1974) American screenwriter who first worked as an airplane pilot and freelance writer during the late 1920s. He began writing original stories and screenplays for action and adventure films in 1937 and continued screenwriting for over twenty years. Page 26.

brunt of, borne the: carried or sustained the heaviest or hardest part of something. From *borne,* carried, sustained, endured, and *brunt,* the heaviest or hardest part. Page 85.

Bubbling Well Road: a well-known street in Shanghai, China, so called from a famous well dating from the third century. The road was later renamed as part of Nanjing Road, Shanghai's principal shopping district. The address 181 Bubbling Well Road refers to the location of a gambling casino. Page 15.

bucked up agin: pushed with effort against something. *Agin* is an informal variation of against. Page 112.

buckskin: a soft, grayish-yellow leather usually having a suede finish, once made from deerskins but now generally made from sheepskins, and used for making clothing. Also items of clothing made from buckskin. Page 8.

Buckskin Brigades: a novel by L. Ron Hubbard, published (1937) by The Macaulay Publishing Company and hailed as a first-ever authentic description of Native North American people and way of life. Set in the early 1800s, the story centers on the Blackfeet Indians, a powerful Native American nation threatened by the fur trade and by white men intent on trapping beaver for the fur, a valuable commodity in Europe. The trappers build forts and organize brigades (convoys of canoes, sleds, wagons or pack animals used to supply trappers), all without regard for either the Indians or the environment. Page 8.

Buffalo Bill: William Frederick Cody (1846–1917), American guide, scout and showman. At the close of the American Civil War in 1865, he contracted with the Kansas Pacific Railroad to furnish buffalo meat to the workers on the line. His claim of killing more than four thousand buffaloes in less than eighteen months earned him the nickname "Buffalo Bill." In 1883 Cody organized his *Wild West Show,* a representation of life on the plains, which toured Europe and the United States for almost twenty years. Page 138.

bumper: a person or thing that serves to lessen shock or impact; a buffer. Page 147.

bunk: nonsense or empty talk. Page 130.

Burks, Arthur J.: (1898–1974) American writer whose enormous output for the pulps included aviation, detective, adventure and horror stories. Page 53.

Burr: John "Jack" Burr, editor of *Western Story* magazine. Page 82.

bush: a large uncleared area thickly covered with mixed plant growth, trees, etc., as a jungle. Page 84.

busies: a word used by science fiction author Robert A. Heinlein (1907–1988) in his best-known work, *Stranger in a Strange Land* (1961), in reference to government operatives who, to accomplish their own ends, interfere in others' affairs. Page 167.

buzzard(s): a slang term for a pilot, especially a pilot of gliders (motorless planes that use upward air currents to stay aloft). A *buzzard* is a large bird that can soar (glide) in the air for many hours using the currents of hot air rising from the ground. Page 15.

Bx.: an abbreviation for *box,* short for *post office box,* a private, numbered box in a post office where mail is held until collected by the addressee. Page 107.

by gum: a variation of *by god,* used to emphasize what one is saying. Page 96.

Byrne, Jack: editor of *Argosy* magazine during the 1930s. Page 7.

by turns: one thing following after another. Page 7.

by way of: by means of; by the route of. Page 20.

C

caballero: a cowboy or horseman, based on the Spanish word *caballo,* horse. Page 82.

calculus: a form of mathematics dealing with things in a state of change. In calculus irregular shapes or varying movement can be calculated. For example, calculus can be used to determine the rate of speed of an accelerating rocket at a given instant, such as exactly twenty seconds after takeoff. Page 13.

California centennial: the three years of celebrations commemorating the one hundredth anniversary (centennial) of three significant events in the history of California: the discovery of gold in 1848, the drafting of the California constitution in 1849 and the acceptance of California as one of the states of the United States in 1850. The centennials were celebrated from 1948 to 1950 and included the establishment of museums, the publishing of books on the history of California and other events. Page 151.

camaraderie: a feeling of close friendship and trust among a particular group of people. Page 27.

Campbell, Jr., John W.: (1910–1971) American editor and writer who began writing science fiction while at college. In 1937 Campbell was appointed editor of the magazine *Astounding Stories,* later titled *Astounding Science Fiction* and then *Analog.* Under his editorship *Astounding* became a major influence in the development of science fiction and published stories by some of the most important writers of that time. Page 2.

can: a slang term for a toilet or bathroom. Page 141.

Canadian border, lost: a reference to a 1931 United States Geological Survey team of which L. Ron Hubbard was a member. The team was to locate damaged or destroyed US/Canada border markers in the northeastern state of Maine to settle the geographic limit of the United States. Page 13.

candor: the quality of being truthful and honest. Page 56.

canned: patterned and unoriginal. From weekly radio and television shows that are recorded in advance for later broadcast, utilizing prerecorded laughter, clapping and other predictable, repetitive elements. Page 130.

Cannondale, Conn.: a town in southern Connecticut, a state in the northeastern United States. Page 12.

Cargo of Coffins: an LRH story first published in *Argosy* magazine in November 1937. In this sea adventure, Lars Martin signs up as captain on an oceangoing yacht where the man who doomed him to a prison colony is also aboard. Page 101.

carriage return: a mechanism in a typewriter, specifically the cylindrical paper holder that, when a key is pressed, moves back after a line is typed. After moving back, the mechanism rotates to move the paper upward, ready to begin a new line. Page 139.

Carroll: Lewis Carroll, pen name of Charles Lutwidge Dodgson (1832–1898), English author, mathematician and photographer, best known for his children's stories, fantastic and completely at odds with reality: *Alice's Adventures in Wonderland* (1865) and its sequel, *Through the Looking-Glass* (1871). Page 129.

Cartier, Edd: Edward Daniel Cartier (1914–2008), American pulp magazine illustrator. From the 1930s to the 1950s, his work regularly appeared in many of the foremost pulp magazines. During the 1990s his lifelong accomplishments were recognized with special awards from fan and professional associations and he further contributed his artistic expertise as a judge of the Illustrators of the Future Contest, starting in its inaugural year. Page 133.

Casanova: the autobiography of Giacomo Casanova (1725–1798), an Italian adventurer, spy, gambler and author. In his *The History of My Life,* Casanova recounts his adventures and affairs, presenting a firsthand look at famous people he knew as well as customs of the period. Page 101.

"Casey Jones": a song first published in 1902 about a well-known and respected US locomotive driver of the same name. The song describes the events leading up to a head-on train collision in April 1900 that took Jones's life. Page 91.

catching: passing from one person to another like an infection or disease. Page 54.

celestial: of the finest or highest kind; heavenly. Page 19.

centennial, California: the three years of celebrations commemorating the one hundredth anniversary (centennial) of three significant events in the history of California: the discovery of gold in 1848, the drafting of the California constitution in 1849 and the acceptance of California as one of the states of the United States in 1850. The centennials were celebrated from 1948 to 1950 and included the establishment of museums, the publishing of books on the history of California and other events. Page 151.

Central Time: the standard time in the zone that includes the central states of the United States and the central provinces of Canada. Page 80.

Chandler, Raymond: (1888–1959) American author of crime and detective stories, mostly set in Los Angeles during the 1930s and 1940s. Page 51.

Chapultepec: a fortress and military school at the outskirts of Mexico City, captured by the US (1847) in the Mexican War (1846–1848). The Marines entered Mexico City and raised the American flag over the National Palace. Page 16.

chawin': a spelling that represents a humorous pronunciation of *chewing*. Page 96.

checklessly: without a check or checks (that is, having no funds). Used humorously. Page 96.

check line: figuratively, where one would line up to receive a check issued as payment of salary or wages. Page 20.

chew (one) off: start and finish (something). Page 147.

chew the fat: talk together in a friendly, leisurely way; chat at length. Page 157.

Chi: an abbreviation for Chicago, the third-largest city in the United States, located in the north central part of the country. Page 156.

chicken paper: a journal of poultry farming. Page 68.

chin-chin: make light, casual conversation with someone; chitchat. Page 156.

choice: well-chosen; selected with care; most appropriate. Page 2.

chronicles: records or recounts, as in a historical record of facts or events in the order they happened. Page 30.

chuck Chuckaluck: *chuckaluck* is a gambling game played with three dice, in which the players bet that a certain number will come up on one die, that the three dice will total a certain number or that the total will be an odd number, even number, a high number or a low number. *Chuck* means throw and here is used with reference to throwing the dice. Hence *chuck Chuckaluck,* play the gambling game of chuckaluck. Page 96.

chuck (one's) weight around: exercise (one's) power or influence, often to an excessive degree; give (one's) opinions (too) freely. In this context, *chuck* means throw and is used somewhat playfully to suggest the throwing of heavy things with ease or contempt; *weight* means influence, power or authority. Page 114.

circumnavigated: bypassed; gotten around; avoided. Page 90.

city ed(itor): the newspaper editor in charge of local news. Page 53.

civil engineer: a person who designs public structures, such as roads, bridges, canals, dams and harbors, or supervises their construction or maintenance. Page 13.

clauses: distinct parts of an official or formal document, covering a particular subject, condition, etc. Page 20.

click: have a sudden recognition of information one had not known before, likened to making a slight, sharp sound, as of pieces coming together. Page 24.

cloying: producing weariness or disgust through too much of something. Page 77.

club sandwiches: sandwiches made of three or more slices of toast, usually with layers of turkey or chicken and bacon or ham, and containing lettuce, tomatoes and mayonnaise. Page 61.

Coast: the North American coast bordering the Pacific Ocean; the West Coast. Page 22.

Coast Guard: the branch of the armed forces that is responsible for coastal defense, protection of life and property at sea, and enforcement of customs, immigration and navigation laws. Page 55.

codger: an informal term for an elderly man. Page 166.

coin phonograph: a coin-operated machine with push buttons for automatically playing selected *records,* flat plastic discs that have music stored on them. Page 141.

Columbia: a university founded in 1754 in New York City, New York. Columbia University is a major institution of higher learning that includes schools and colleges of arts and sciences, engineering, medicine and business. Page 153.

Columbia (Pictures): a motion picture studio established in Hollywood, California, during the 1920s, becoming one of the largest US film companies. Page 7.

column: a regular article by a particular writer that appears regularly in a newspaper, often an article that is also sold to other newspapers for publication in a number of areas. Page 53.

Commander of the Legion of Honor: the middle rank of five levels awarded by the Legion of Honor (a French honorary society founded by Napoleon in 1802) for outstanding achievements in military or civil life. Page 56.

commentatin': *commenting,* expressing an opinion about, or a reaction to, something. Page 96.

condemned: used to intensify a statement of one's annoyance about someone or something. Page 158.

Conquest of Space: a series of nine LRH stories that first appeared in *Startling Stories* magazine (published by Standard Magazines) between 1948 and 1950. The stories are based on information obtained from archives in the future—after Man has conquered space—that deal with the human barriers that Man must overcome to reach the stars. Page 156.

Conquistadores: Spanish conquerors of Mexico and Peru in the sixteenth century. Page 13.

contention: a statement or point that one argues for as true. Page 66.

continuity: a comprehensive script for a motion picture, laid out in the order in which scenes are to be shown on the screen, that includes full details of the contents of each scene, including items such as camera positions, settings, costume features and the like. Page 74.

contometer: a device for calculating the number of words typed, based on the number of keystrokes on a typewriter. Based on the *comptometer,* a type of adding machine that was invented in the late 1800s. Page 114.

contract: an agreement between two or more people for the doing or not doing of something specified (sometimes signed and enforceable by law). Page 20.

copious: large in quantity or number; abundant. Page 114.

corvette: a lightly armed, fast ship used especially during World War II (1939–1945) to accompany a group of supply ships and protect them from attack by enemy submarines. Page 145.

Cosmo: short for *Cosmopolitan* magazine. Page 135.

cosmopolitan: not local, limited or restricted by the attitudes, interests, loyalties or prejudices of a single region, section or sphere of activity; at home all over the world. Page 15.

costume (novel): a novel set during a specific period in history and including authentic characters, scenes and descriptions. Page 11.

courtesy of: given by (someone). Page 2.

cover(s): a thing that provides sufficient funds or that is a means of guaranteed income to meet one's expenses. Page 147.

Crabtown: a nickname for Baltimore, Maryland, where crab from the Chesapeake Bay is a famous delicacy. Page 13.

crafting: making or creating (something) using special skills. Page 2.

cramp (one's) style: restrain from free expression of one's tastes or skill; dampen the spirits of. Page 18.

Crime and Punishment: a novel by Russian author Feodor Mikhailovich Dostoyevsky (1821–1881) about a poor student, Raskolnikov, who, worried about his poverty and helpless family, murders an old woman and takes her money. Despite his attempts to justify his actions, guilt eats at him until he finally confesses and is sent to prison. With deep psychological insight, Dostoyevsky realistically portrays the conflicting desires of the characters in their struggle between good and evil. Page 153.

crooked: doing things that are illegal; dishonest. Page 107.

Crosby, Bing: (1903–1977) popular American singer and motion picture star. His more than one thousand records have sold over three hundred million copies and he also appeared in more than fifty films. Page 112.

cross-barred S: the symbol for the United States dollar, which is written as an S with a line through it ($). *Cross-barred* means marked with lines or stripes. Page 27.

crude oil: literally, petroleum as it occurs naturally; also a pun involving the word *crude,* offensively coarse or rude. Page 53.

cryptographer: one who uses, develops or studies systems and techniques of secret writing, codes, etc. Page 159.

curled: raised the upper corner of the lip, as in showing contempt or scorn. Page 20.

cuss: an informal word for *curse,* use swear words in one's conversation. Page 19.

cussed: an informal word meaning stubborn and uncooperative. Page 166.

cutback: a sequence of earlier events introduced at a later point in a story, novel, film, etc. Page 32.

cyclometer: a type of device for adding up the number of keystrokes on a typewriter, based on mechanical motion. Also called *stroke counter*. Page 114.

cyows: a spelling that represents a humorous pronunciation of *cows*. Page 96.

czar: one having great power or authority in a particular field, from the former emperors of Russia, who ruled with complete authority. Page 40.

D

dabbled: took part in an activity in a casual way, not seriously. From the literal meaning of *dabble,* move (one's hands or feet) around gently in water. Page 98.

dame(s): an informal term for a woman or girl. Page 25.

dang: an informal way of saying *damn,* used for emphasis. Page 112.

dashing: characterized by prompt vigor of action; impetuous, spirited, lively. Page 95.

Daudet: Alphonse Daudet (1840–1897), French author, often compared to English writer Charles Dickens for his short stories and novels, which recorded the social problems of his period. Film adaptations in the 1930s and 1950s brought his works to the screen. *See also* **Dickens.** Page 129.

Dead Men Kill: an LRH story first published in *Thrilling Detective* magazine in July 1934. A detective investigating a series of murders finds himself battling corpses that carry the smell of damp earth and undertakers. Page 86.

deaf ear, turn a: refuse to listen to or consider. Page 65.

Death's Deputy: an LRH story first published in *Unknown* magazine in February 1940. When people mysteriously begin to die around Clayton McLean, he knows their deaths are somehow related to him. Page 119.

de Camp, L. Sprague: (1907–2000) American writer who produced works of fantasy, nonfiction, fiction and science fiction during a sixty-year literary career. Page 136.

deep, (five thousand): completed to the amount of (five thousand words). Page 138.

defining: showing the distinctive character of something. Page 1.

de la Falaise de la Coudray, Marquis: Henri Marquis de la Falaise de la Coudray (1898–1972), French nobleman, translator, film director, film producer and war hero. In his 1935 motion picture *Kliou the Killer,* filmed on location in the jungles of Vietnam, a young man volunteers to track down a man-eating tiger that has been terrorizing his people. Page 84.

Dell: Dell Publishing Company, one of the major pulp magazine publishing companies during the early twentieth century; later, a major publisher of paperback books. Page 54.

Department of Justice: an executive department of the United States Government. It enforces federal laws and provides legal advice for the president and the heads of the government's other executive departments. One of the largest agencies within the Department of Justice is the FBI (Federal Bureau of Investigation), which investigates violations of federal laws. Page 86.

depression: a period marked by slackening of business activity, increased unemployment, falling prices and wages, etc., particularly the economic crisis and period of low business activity in the United States and other countries, roughly beginning with the stock market crash in October 1929 and continuing through most of the 1930s. Page 63.

depths, doggy: a point of extremely low spirits, as from dealing with failure. From a slang meaning of *dog,* something that is a failure. Page 103.

Detective Fiction Weekly: a pulp magazine that published some nine hundred issues in all, from the early 1920s until the early 1950s, containing stories by many of the best-known authors of stories for the pulp magazines. Page 7.

DFW: an abbreviation for *Detective Fiction Weekly* magazine. Page 22.

Dianetics: Dianetics is a forerunner and substudy of Scientology. Dianetics means "through the mind" or "through the soul" (from Greek *dia,* through, and *nous,* mind or soul). It is a system of coordinated axioms which resolve problems concerning human behavior and psychosomatic illnesses. It combines a workable technique and a thoroughly validated method for increasing sanity, by erasing unwanted sensations and unpleasant emotions. Page 1.

Dickens: Charles Dickens (1812–1870), prolific English novelist of the mid-nineteenth century whose books are noted for picturesque and extravagant characters in the lower economic strata of England. Page 99.

dictaphone: a *dictating machine,* a machine for recording dictation, as on cassettes or disks, for subsequent transcription. Page 145.

dime novel: an inexpensive sensational paperback novel, popular around the mid-1800s to the early 1900s and originally costing a dime (US coin equal to ten cents). Page 55.

dish roulette: *roulette* is a gambling game in which a small ball is rolled onto a spinning horizontal wheel. The wheel is curved inward, like a dish, and is divided into numbered compartments. Players bet on which compartment the ball will come to rest in. *Dish* means serve something by placing it into a dish and here is used figuratively with reference to rolling the small ball onto the roulette wheel. Hence *dish roulette,* play the gambling game of roulette. Page 96.

dispensation: official authorization, granting the right to do some action or an exemption from a usual requirement or rule. Page 25.

division: a self-contained unit of an army capable of sustained operations, consisting of some thousands of troops and a headquarters. Hence a *Turkish division,* a unit in the Turkish army during World War I (1914–1919). Page 56.

do and die: a variation of *do-or-die,* a phrase used to express determination not to be stopped by any difficulty or danger. Page 15.

docket: a writing on a letter or document stating its contents; any statement of particulars attached to a package, envelope, etc.; a label or ticket. Page 9.

Dod: a mild expression of upset, irritation or the like (a deliberate alteration of *God*). Page 157.

doggy depths: a point of extremely low spirits, as from dealing with failure. From a slang meaning of *dog,* something that is a failure. Page 103.

dolorous: very sorrowful or sad; mournful. Page 133.

Don: in Spanish-speaking countries, a gentleman; also a title (corresponding to Mr. or Sir) used in front of a man's first name. Page 82.

dope: a slang term for information, data or news. Page 68.

Dostoyevsky: Feodor Mikhailovich Dostoyevsky (1821–1881), Russian novelist and short-story writer whose writings often included the human potential for evil, such as the brutality of prison guards who enjoyed cruelty for its own sake, the evil of criminals who could enjoy murdering children, as well as the existence of decent individuals amid filth and degradation. The underlying theme in his books is the struggle between good and evil for dominance of the human soul. Page 129.

double howl: a *howl* is a yell or outcry of disappointment, anger or protest. *Double* means having a twofold relation or character. Thus a *double howl* refers to a situation causing outcries of disappointment, anger or protest from two places or on two counts. Page 55.

down to: in or into a position or place thought of as inferior or a lower status. Page 55.

drawn and quartered: a reference to the death penalty given to a person in England prior to the fifteenth century, usually for a major crime. The sentence had slight variations but basically consisted of dragging the person behind a horse to the site of execution, hanging him briefly, cutting open his stomach and removing his internal organs (drawing), beheading him and then chopping the body into four pieces (quartering) and putting the parts on spikes in public places to serve as an example. Page 34.

drill along: make steady progress forward in a straight line as if driven with a *drill,* a tool for making holes in hard substances. Page 138.

drop in (on): pay an informal visit or call. Page 21.

Dunsany, Lord: Edward John Moreton Drax Plunkett Dunsany (1878–1957), Irish poet, dramatist and novelist. Many of his writings deal with "the mysterious kingdoms where geography ends and fairyland begins." Dunsany employed this background to satirize human behavior in a simple, charming style. Page 42.

Durant: a city in southern Oklahoma, a state in the south central United States, established in the mid-1800s. Page 81.

E

earning (one's) bread: receiving money as payment for work that one does in order to be able to purchase food, clothes and other ordinary needs. Page 54.

ebb(s), at low: a point or condition of gradual decline from a higher to a lower level (as of activity) or from a better to a worse state. From the movement of the tide (the periodic rise and fall of the level of water in the ocean), with the ebb being the action of the water flowing away from the shore and going back out to sea. Page 76.

Echols, Al: Allan K. Echols, a prolific writer for the pulps in the 1930s–1950s. His stories included numerous westerns as well as science fiction, detective and adventure. Page 68.

ed(s): short for *editor.* Page 56.

Egtvedt: C. L. Egtvedt (1892–1975), president of Boeing Aircraft Company (1933–1939). Page 114.

eighteen gallon hat: a humorous term for a very large cowboy hat, even larger than the usual *ten gallon hat,* one having a high, round, uncreased crown and a wide brim. Page 98.

election period: the time during which members of a community elect (vote for) representatives who will hold a position of authority within it, such as leaders of local, state or national government. In the United States, national elections are held on the first Tuesday after the first Monday in November in even-numbered years. Page 31.

Ellsworth, Fanny: editor of pulp fiction magazines. Besides the long-running *Ranch Romances,* which Ellsworth headed from the 1920s until the early 1950s, she also edited the detective magazine *Black Mask* during the late 1930s. Page 8.

embattle: make (oneself) ready for conflict; be prepared to fight. Page 109.

emblazoned: decorated or adorned with (a design, symbol or the like). Page 27.

emery, put the nose to: work hard and steadily without rest, a variation of *put one's nose to the grindstone.* A *grindstone* is a revolving stone wheel used for polishing or sharpening things, while *emery,* a powdered mineral used as an abrasive, is often coated onto a rotating wheel for the same purpose. Both phrases allude to someone who, hard at work polishing something, bends over with his nose very close to his work. Page 129.

emote: show or express emotion. Page 133.

Encinitas: a coastal town in Southern California, established in the late 1800s. Page 98.

encrusting: concealing or obscuring (something) as if with a layer or crust. Page 77.

End Is Not Yet, The: an LRH story first published in *Astounding Science Fiction* magazine as a three-part series, appearing in the August, September and October 1947 issues. The setting is a dangerous postatomic world, where a conspiracy to provoke a nuclear war is defeated by a coalition of scientists. Page 152.

enroute: on the way. Page 151.

ensconced: established in a place or position. Page 7.

entranced: filled with delight; charmed with. Page 91.

epistle: a formal term for a letter, especially a long, formal, instructive letter. Used humorously. Page 114.

epistol: a playful spelling of *epistle* and a play on the word *pistol. See also* **pistol.** Page 99.

Erasmus: Desiderius Erasmus (1466?–1536), Dutch priest and scholar who sought to reform the Church. Page 104.

Esq.: an abbreviation for *esquire,* a chiefly British term appended to a man's name as a polite title when no other title is used, especially in a letter. Page 12.

essayed: tried or attempted. Page 91.

esthetic: also *aesthetic,* having or showing an appreciation of things that are beautiful or pleasing. Page 90.

et al.: abbreviation for the Latin phrase *et alia,* meaning "and others." Page 104.

ethnological: of or having to do with *ethnology,* the science that analyzes cultures, especially in regard to their historical development and the similarities and dissimilarities between them. Page 119.

ethnologist: someone trained and specializing in ethnology. *See also* **ethnological.** Page 32.

even break: a fair chance. Page 55.

eyesore: something that is unpleasant or offensively ugly to look at. Page 91.

F
___

face, give it some: present (a matter) in a way that is appropriate and that gives the best impression. Page 153.

"Face on the Barroom Floor, The": a popular American ballad based on a poem written in 1877. The song tells the story of a successful artist who, when his true love runs off with another man, becomes a penniless drunk. While begging for drinks in a bar, the artist proceeds to draw his sweetheart's face on the barroom floor. Page 90.

faction: a group of people who are part of a larger group and have specific interests that conflict with other such groups. Page 34.

factory hands: people engaged in manual labor in a *factory,* a building or buildings where goods are manufactured or assembled chiefly by machine. Page 53.

fallout: airborne radioactive dust and material shot into the atmosphere by a nuclear explosion which then settles to the ground. *Radioactive* describes a substance that sends out harmful energy in the form of streams of very small particles due to the decay (breaking down) of atoms within the substance. Page 166.

fambly: a spelling that represents a humorous pronunciation of *family.* Page 112.

Famine, Death, Pestilence: a reference to the Biblical description of the evils that will come at the end of the world, symbolized by the Four Horsemen who ride white, red, black and pale horses, symbolizing pestilence, war, famine and death, respectively. (*Pestilence* is an epidemic of a highly contagious fatal disease, such as the plague, that kills many people.) Page 107.

fan dancer: a woman who does a *fan dance,* where the performer is nude or nearly nude and uses fans for covering. Page 107.

Fantasy Pub(lishing): Fantasy Publishing Company, Inc., a California book-publishing company that operated from the mid-1940s to the early 1970s. Fantasy Publishing specialized in science fiction and fantasy publications. Page 156.

far-flung: extended far or to a great distance; remote. Page 1.

farm, down on the: at home; the place where someone is located or residing. Page 112.

fastidious: displaying very careful attention to detail. Page 90.

faze: cause (someone) to be disturbed or worried about something. Page 75.

feather in (one's) cap: an act or achievement that gives (someone) cause to be proud. Page 20.

fell to: began (to do a specified action). Page 74.

fencing with: exchanging words with (someone), as in an argument. Page 2.

fergot: a spelling that represents a humorous pronunciation of *forgot*. Page 158.

Finn, James J.: a New York City police detective, noted for his thorough and detailed investigation into the kidnapping and murder of Charles Lindbergh's baby son. *See also* **Hauptmann.** Page 85.

fire, on the: being worked on. Page 47.

first crack out: at the first opportunity; before anything else; immediately. From *get a crack at,* an expression that refers to someone getting a shot at an animal, as in hunting. *Crack* here means an opportunity or attempt. Page 62.

fits and starts, in: do in short bursts of activity, repeated in stops and starts. (A *fit* is a sudden, short-lived state of activity or inactivity. A *start* is a brief, sudden movement or action from being still.) Page 151.

five-lunged crate: a rickety and dilapidated airplane having five cylinders. A *cylinder* is a chamber in an engine in which the fuel and air are combined. When the fuel is ignited, the explosion generates the power that makes the engine run. Page 15.

Five-Novels Monthly: a pulp magazine published from 1928 until the late 1940s. The monthly schedule was continued until 1943, when paper shortages during World War II (1939–1945) forced it to a quarterly schedule and a resultant name change to *Five Novels* magazine. Page 2.

flagged: lessened in vigor, energy, activity, interest, etc. Page 160.

flag waving: an excessive and emotional display of patriotism. Page 16.

fledglings: inexperienced persons just starting on their careers. Page 2.

Fletcher: Murray Fletcher Pratt (1897–1956), American writer of science fiction, fantasy and naval history, particularly on the American Civil War. Page 136.

flooey: in a disordered state. Page 156.

Florence: Florence McChesney, editor of *Five-Novels Monthly.* Page 18.

flush: having plenty of money. Page 156.

flyeth: a poetic way of saying something passes swiftly, as in *"time flyeth."* Page 141.

flying fortress: an informal name for the Boeing B-17, an American long-range heavy bomber airplane developed in the late 1930s. Page 114.

FN: an abbreviation for *Five-Novels Monthly* magazine. Page 24.

footsore: having sore feet from much walking. Page 51.

foray: an exploration into something. Page 8.

forbear: avoid or refrain from doing something. Page 90.

Forrest: Forrest "Forry" Ackerman, Los Angeles literary agent and editor, specializing in science fiction and fantasy. Page 77.

forte: strong point; a particularly good quality or characteristic. Page 68.

49 book: a book related to the then-upcoming 1949 celebration of the California centennial. *See also* **California centennial.** Page 147.

fray, to the: to a situation of intense activity, from the literal meaning of *fray,* a battle or fight. Page 103.

freight, pulling (one's): taking off or leaving with (one's) luggage. From the sense of *freight,* items being carried, and *pull,* move or proceed by use of force, as in moving goods from one place to another. Page 27.

French Foreign Legion: a unit of the French army, one of the most famous fighting forces in the world. Formed in 1831, the Foreign Legion consists of eight thousand men who apply for duty and are generally accepted regardless of background or occupation and must come from a country other than France. Page 16.

front office: the executive or administrative office of a company, organization, etc. Page 140.

fruition: attainment of something desired or worked for; accomplishment. Page 1.

G

gabbed: chattered or spoken in an idle, rapid or thoughtless manner, especially at length. Page 130.

gallantry: heroic bravery, especially in war or in a situation of great danger; nobility of spirit or action. Page 91.

Galsworthy: John Galsworthy (1867–1933), English novelist and playwright. His fiction is concerned principally with English upper-middle-class life. Several of his works were adapted for motion pictures and he won the Nobel Prize in Literature in 1932. Page 78.

gamut: entire range of something. Page 26.

Garcia, message to: a reference to the essay "Message to Garcia" by American author and editor Elbert Hubbard (1856–1915). Originally published in 1899, it tells the story of an American soldier named Rowan who, during the Spanish-American War (1898), was asked by the president of the United States to deliver a crucial message to the Cuban rebel leader, Garcia, in Cuba. Against enormous odds, the message was delivered and the account by Elbert Hubbard, published in one of his magazines, attained enduring popularity due to its moral: no matter what odds one faces in the performance of duty, one must carry out his assigned task, one must carry his message to Garcia. Page 106.

garret: a small, uncomfortable room just below the roof of a house, also called an *attic*. The word *garret* is often used in reference to the lifestyle of a writer or artist who, trying to make a living at his art, lives and works in such quarters and goes without food because he has no money. Page 63.

Genghis Khan: (1162–1227) Mongolian general and emperor. He conquered large portions of China and southwestern Asia. His army ruthlessly eliminated any enemy; they were known to systematically slaughter the population of entire cities that resisted them. Page 51.

genre(s): a category of artistic composition, as in music or literature, marked by a distinctive style, form or content. Page 1.

gent(s): a gentleman. Page 68.

Geological Survey: the United States Geological Survey is the nation's largest water, earth science, biological science and civilian mapping agency. The Geological Survey collects, monitors, analyzes and provides scientific information about natural resource conditions, issues and problems. Page 13.

Geopolitick: a German word meaning *geopolitics,* the study and analysis of political relations among nations, especially as they involve claims and disputes pertaining to borders, territories, etc. The Nazis used the concept to justify German expansionism. Page 157.

ghoulash: a humorous spelling of *goulash,* the name of a stew of Hungarian origin. *Goulash* also means an uncoordinated mixture of something; a mishmash or jumble. A *ghoul* is an evil spirit or demon in Middle-Eastern legends believed to rob graves and feed on corpses. Page 130.

Ghoul, The: an LRH story first published in *Unknown* magazine in August 1939. An inquisitive hotel employee opens a trunk left by a mysterious turbaned guest, but finds it empty. And then the voices begin... (A *ghoul* is an evil spirit or demon in Middle-Eastern legends believed to rob graves and feed on corpses.) Page 47.

gift of gab: a special ability or talent for using words fluently or eloquently. Page 129.

gilded-gingerbread: elaborately embellished or enhanced with inessential but decorative or fanciful details. *Gilded* means overlaid with a thin covering of gold. *Gingerbread* here means showy and elaborate decoration. Page 79.

Ginny: Virginia Heinlein (1916–2003), wife of author Robert A. Heinlein. Page 157.

git up and go: a spelling that represents an informal pronunciation of *get up and go,* driving ambition; vigor; energy. Page 166.

G-men: agents for the Federal Bureau of Investigation. *G* is an abbreviation of *government.* Page 69.

Gnu Yawk: a spelling that represents a humorous pronunciation of the name *New York,* in imitation of a New York City accent. Page 138.

good, all to the: having the required qualities; of a high standard. Page 103.

go-to-hell: characterized by a willingness to go through any disagreeable, troublesome, stirring or exciting experience to accomplish an objective. Page 16.

graced: favored or honored. Page 1.

grade B+: good or above average in quality, from the system used in schools in the United States and other countries to indicate the quality of a student's work. Page 45.

grade C+: average in quality, from the system used in schools in the United States and other countries to indicate the quality of a student's work. Page 45.

granary foundation: figuratively, the basis of one's literary output. A *granary* is a warehouse or storeroom for grain. The slang term for a typewriter is a *mill,* a word that also means a building equipped with machinery for grinding grain into flour. A *granary* would therefore be a storehouse of material that can be turned into literary works. Page 108.

Grand Coulee Dam: a dam on the Columbia River in Washington State. It is one of the largest concrete structures in the world and a major source of electric power. Page 108.

graveled: irritated or annoyed. Page 158.

gray matter: literally, the grayish tissue of the brain and spinal cord, consisting chiefly of nerve cells. Used informally to mean intellectual capacity; brains. Page 104.

greased pig: the object of a *greased pig chase,* a tradition at some country gatherings in which a small pig greased with vegetable oil or the like is chased around a fenced area. The pig is very hard to catch because it can move fast and especially because it is made slippery. Used here figuratively to indicate that someone is very unreliable (greasy or slippery), even more than a pig covered with grease. Page 158.

Great Dallas Strudemeyer: a proposed pen name for LRH. Page 156.

great guns: in an extremely energetic way. Page 135.

Great Northern: the Great Northern Railroad, a 1,700-mile (2,736-kilometer) railway that began construction in the late 1800s. It eventually extended from the western end of Lake Superior in central North America, north to just below the Canadian border, through Minnesota, Montana and Idaho and on to Puget Sound, Washington. During the 1930s the Great Northern advertised its route, employing artists to portray Blackfeet Indians and scenes of the West. Page 39.

greener, make the field: make something better, richer, fuller, more remunerative, etc., likened to making a field greener for better grazing. Page 80.

greener pastures: a place or activity regarded as offering new opportunities. Page 79.

griddle, on the: in progress; not yet completed. (From the idea of being cooked on a *griddle,* a heavy flat, metal plate or pan for cooking.) Page 149.

grisly: characterized by a feeling of horror. Page 84.

Gruber, Frank: (1904–1969) American writer best known for his westerns and detective stories. He wrote some three hundred stories as well as more than sixty novels and two hundred screenplays and television scripts. Page 68.

Guam: an island in the northwestern Pacific Ocean, a territory of the United States and site of US air and naval bases. Page 14.

gum, by: a variation of *by god,* used to emphasize what one is saying. Page 96.

gummed: covered with a sticky (gummy) substance, as from the plants found in a swamp. Page 13.

gumshoe(s): an informal term for a detective, especially a private investigator, from the idea of moving quietly and with stealth, as if wearing *gumshoes,* sneakers with a rubber sole or rubber overshoes. Page 66.

gunslinger: during the frontier days of the American West, a person who was skilled in using a gun and was employed for protection or to kill people. Page 80.

H

habituated: accustomed to, familiarized with. Page 148.

Hammett, Dashiell: (1894–1961) highly influential American author of detective novels. Drawing on his years of work as a private detective, Hammett began writing in the early 1920s. With his realistic writing style, he created enduringly popular characters and plots, with a number of his best-known works, such as *The Maltese Falcon* (1930), later adapted for film. Page 51.

hand over fist: at a tremendous rate. From the way sailors haul in or climb up a rope. Page 36.

hands down: without question; unconditionally. Page 68.

handsome: 1. having many admirable qualities. Page 13.
2. having a pleasing appearance; well made and of obvious quality. Page 90.

handsomely: successfully; in good style; pleasingly. Page 90.

hard-boiled: down-to-earth, practical, realistic; tough; not affected by sentiment, pity, etc. Page 22.

Harpers Ferry: a village in eastern West Virginia, on the Potomac River, 55 miles (89 kilometers) northwest of Washington, DC, site of a federal arsenal. When the arsenal was captured by antislavery campaigner John Brown and his followers (October 1859), Marines from Washington, DC, were the only troops available. They helped capture Brown and occupied the arsenal. *See also* **Brown, John.** Page 16.

hash house: an inexpensive restaurant. Page 62.

Hassan, Silaki Ali: a pseudonym of writer Ulysses George Mihalakis, author of science fiction stories, including "Caliph of Yafri," which appeared in the September 1939 issue of *Unknown.* Page 45.

hassled: bothered, annoyed or harassed. Page 167.

Hauptmann: Bruno Richard Hauptmann (1899–1936), a burglar who was convicted of the 1932 kidnapping and murder of aviator Charles Lindbergh's baby son. Page 85.

Havana: capital, port and largest city of Cuba, on the northwestern coast of the country. Cuba is the largest and westernmost island of the West Indies. Page 136.

hear tell: am told (of something); have received information (about something). Page 20.

heart set on, has (one's): has a fixed desire for; wishes for intensely; wants. Page 141.

heart-throbber: an informal term for a story about love and romance, so called because it makes the heart *throb,* beat rapidly. Page 8.

heat lift: an upward force exerted on part of the surface of an aircraft by currents of warm air that rise through the cooler surrounding air. Such air flows help the aircraft stay in the air. Page 15.

heels: a reference to dishonorable or irresponsible people, an offensive term used to deliberately insult somebody's, especially a man's, behavior. Page 71.

Heinlein, Robert: (1907–1988) American author considered one of the most important writers of science fiction. Emerging during science fiction's Golden Age (1939–1949), Heinlein went on to write many novels, including the classic *Stranger in a Strange Land* (1961). He won four Hugo Awards and was presented with the first Grand Master Nebula Award for lifetime achievement in science fiction. Page 2.

Heliplane: an aircraft combining the rotating blade of a helicopter (enabling vertical motion) and the wings and propellers of an airplane (for efficient, high-speed forward motion). Page 98.

he-man: a strong, tough, forceful man. Page 11.

Hemingway: Ernest Hemingway (1899–1961), American novelist and short-story writer, a number of whose stories addressed social issues, as in *For Whom the Bell Tolls* (1940) about the Spanish Civil War. Many of Hemingway's works are regarded as classics of American literature. Page 51.

Henry, O.: pen name of William Sydney Porter (1862–1910), American short-story writer noted for his mastery of plot twists that build to an unexpected ending. In the 1890s, Porter served three years in prison in Columbus, Ohio, after being charged with embezzling funds. It was here he began to write short stories and use the pen name O. Henry. Page 82.

hermit: any person living in seclusion. Page 22.

hiatus: a break or interruption in work or action. Page 145.

"Highwayman, The": a famous poem and song about the eighteenth-century English highwayman Dick Turpin. In the tragic poem, Turpin's lover is captured by British troops in an attempt to capture the highwayman, but she shoots and kills herself in order to warn Turpin of the plot, allowing him to make an escape. (A *highwayman* was a man, typically on horseback, who robbed travelers.) Page 91.

hillbilly: a person from a backwoods or other remote area, especially from the mountains of the southern United States. Page 124.

hither and yon: in this direction and in that (alternately); to and fro; in various directions. Page 147.

hitherto: up to this time; until now. Page 53.

hock shop: a slang term for a *pawnshop,* a place that lends money at interest in exchange for personal property deposited as security. Page 109.

holding out: withholding something expected or due. Page 54.

honey-comb quartz: *quartz,* a brilliant, crystalline mineral, often found in conjunction with gold. Some forms of quartz appear as crystals in which each crystal has six sides, like the individual cells of a honey-comb (a wax structure made by bees to store honey and eggs). Page 15.

horse in town is located on a whiskey bottle, only: a humorous reference to a brand of Scotch whiskey called *White Horse,* the label of which shows an image of a horse. Page 68.

hoss(es): a spelling that represents an informal or humorous pronunciation of *horse*. Page 68.

huddling: a meeting together to discuss, exchange ideas, make a decision or the like. Page 2.

Hudson Bay: a large inland sea in northern Canada, 850 miles (1,370 kilometers) long and 600 miles (965 kilometers) wide. It is named for the English explorer Henry Hudson (?–1611), who reached it in 1610, on his fourth voyage to the New World. Page 71.

Hudson's Bay Company: a fur-trading company originally established by English merchants in 1670 for the purpose of trade and settlement in the Hudson Bay region in northeast Canada. Page 30.

hunch: a feeling or guess that something will happen or may be the case. Page 31.

I

iambic pentameter: the most common rhythm in English poetry, in which each line consists of five iambs. An *iamb* is a unit of rhythm in poetry consisting of one unstressed syllable followed by one stressed syllable. "The ploughman homeward plods his weary way" is in iambic pentameter. Page 77.

IBM: *International Business Machines Corporation,* one of the largest manufacturers of business machines during the early and mid-1900s and, later, a manufacturer of the first large-scale computers. Page 26.

imbibe: take in food or liquid through the mouth. Also, take in and assimilate something mentally, such as an idea or experience. Page 89.

incidental: happening as a result of or in connection with something more important. Page 18.

indicting: a playful spelling of *inditing,* expressing in writing; writing down. Page 114.

Indies: a shortened form of *West Indies,* a large group of islands between North America and South America in the North Atlantic. Page 136.

Indigestible Triton, The: an LRH story first published in *Unknown Fantasy Fiction* magazine in April 1940. This classic fantasy tale finds Bill Grayson, on a brief fishing trip, hooking an out-of-the-ordinary fish that turns out to be Trigon, the Triton, great-grandson of Neptune, ruler of the sea. Page 129.

indigo: a deep purplish-blue color. Used here to refer to something characterized by or full of sadness and depression, from the use of the word *blue,* meaning sad. Page 138.

Indochina: the peninsula of Southeast Asia, particularly the portion that was formerly a French colony and that now includes the independent countries of Cambodia, Laos and Vietnam. Page 84.

inertia: a reference to one of the three laws formulated by English scientist and mathematician Sir Isaac Newton (1642–1727). The law of inertia states that: a body at rest remains at rest and a body in motion remains in motion unless acted on by an external force. Page 104.

infallible: something that is unfailing in effectiveness or is certain. Page 107.

infamously: in a way that is *infamous,* well known for some bad quality. Page 40.

Ingraham, Colonel Prentiss: (1843–1904) American military officer and writer. He traveled in the company of Buffalo Bill, the organizer of the *Wild West Show,* a representation of life on the plains that toured Europe and the United States for almost twenty years. Ingraham's stories recount his adventures in the military and on the American frontier. Page 55.

ingrate: somebody who does not show or express gratitude. Page 37.

ingratiate: make (something) pleasant, agreeable, acceptable, etc., to someone. Page 90.

injunction: an earnest warning. Page 34.

Inky: an affectionate name used by LRH for the electric typewriter he used as a writer. Page 124.

intelligence: data or information communicated and/or received. Page 89.

interaction: a reference to one of the three laws of motion formulated by English scientist and mathematician, Sir Isaac Newton (1642–1727). The law of interaction deals with the forces of action and reaction (the two forces that make up the interaction between two objects): Whenever one object exerts a force on a second object, the second object exerts an equal and opposite force on the first. Page 104.

intercedence: the action of speaking in support of somebody involved in a dispute. Page 35.

inter-plot: a story line that occurs between other parts of a novel, play, etc. Page 32.

"Interstate Iniquity Association": a humorous made-up name. *Interstate* means occurring between, connecting or involving two or more states of the United States. *Iniquity* means wrongful action or conduct. Page 137.

intimate: suggest or hint that something is a certain way. Page 21.

iota: the least or a very small quantity. Page 75.

irascible: easily angered; quick-tempered. Page 2.

Iron Duke, The: an LRH story first published in *Five-Novels Monthly* magazine in July 1940. Blackie Lee's outrageous impersonation of the drunken Archduke of Aldoria—with the secret collaboration of the prime minister—leads to unexpected political and personal consequences. Page 138.

Iroquois: a member of a former association or alliance of six Native North American peoples that originally lived in New York, USA, and Ontario, Canada. Page 35.

Irving, Washington: (1783–1859) American writer and one of the first whose works received recognition in Europe as well as in the United States. Besides his well-known stories *Rip Van Winkle* and *The Legend of Sleepy Hollow,* Irving also wrote stories of his travels in the American West and in Europe as well as historical works on figures such as George Washington and Christopher Columbus. Page 41.

Ivanhoe: a historical novel about the Middle Ages, written in 1819 by Scottish author Sir Walter Scott (1771–1832). Page 53.

ivory tower: a place or condition of separation or seclusion from the world and its real-life problems. (The term *ivory tower* originated with the French literary critic Charles-Augustin Sainte-Beuve [1804–1869], who described a poet, Count Alfred-Victor de Vigny [1797–1863], as living in an ivory tower, i.e., isolated from the harsh realities of life.) Page 77.

J

jade: a bad-tempered or immoral woman. Page 19.

jag: a period of overindulgence in an activity; a spree; a binge. Page 83.

jar: a discordant (considered disagreeable to the ear) sound or combination of sounds. Page 112.

jell: something, such as a piece of writing, that has *jelled,* achieved distinctness; taken proper shape and form. Page 107.

"Jesse James": a song about a US outlaw of the same name. James (1847–1882) was notorious for a string of bank and train robberies throughout the West over a period of fifteen years. He was shot in the back and killed by one of his fellow gang members in 1882. Page 90.

Jesse James series: a series of stories published in the late 1800s and early 1900s by Street & Smith. Known as the *Jesse James Stories,* these weekly publications featured fictional tales of the famous outlaw and his gang. Page 134.

jittery: marked by nervousness, a feeling of fright or uneasiness. Page 2.

job: an informal term for a particular kind of object, especially a manufactured item, such as a vehicle. Page 151.

Johnny: John W. Campbell, Jr. *See also* **Campbell, Jr., John W.** Page 123.

johnny cake: a cake or bread made of cornmeal and water or milk, usually cooked on a griddle (a heavy, flat, metal plate or pan for cooking on). Page 13.

John W.: John W. Campbell, Jr. *See also* **Campbell, Jr., John W.** Page 158.

Jonah: a person or thing whose presence is supposed to bring misfortune and bad luck. From the Biblical story of Jonah, who refused to accept a mission given to him by God and instead tried to run away by leaving on a sea voyage. God then raised a great storm as a sign of his anger with Jonah. Seeing that their ship was about to sink and realizing that Jonah's disobedience was the cause of the storm, the sailors threw him overboard in an attempt to save their ship. Page 123.

jot, not a: not the slightest or least amount. From *jot,* a letter of the Greek alphabet (also called *iota*), which is represented in the English alphabet as either the letter *i* (the smallest letter in the alphabet) or the letter *j.* Page 26.

juice: an informal term for electricity or electric power. Page 141.

K
***

Kaintucky: a spelling that represents an informal pronunciation of *Kentucky,* a state in the east central United States. Page 135.

Kansas: a state in the western part of the central US known for its extreme, and variable, weather conditions, including blizzards, hailstorms, thunderstorms and tornadoes. Page 95.

keeping tab on: observing; checking on. Page 126.

Kellogg Company: the world's largest manufacturer of ready-to-eat breakfast cereals. Formed in 1906 by William Keith Kellogg, some years after his brother Dr. John Harvey Kellogg accidentally invented the first flaked cereal while preparing food for his patients, the company was first called the Battle Creek Toasted Corn Flake Company. With successful advertising, the company grew quickly and by 1911 had an advertising budget of over $1 million. Renamed the Kellogg Company in 1922, the company continued to expand with cereal plants established all over the world and more than fifty breakfast cereals and convenience foods produced. Page 88.

kicking: rebelling; expressing discontent; complaining. Page 141.

Kilkenny Cats: one of the stories in the series of the same name, a group of five LRH stories first published in *Astounding Science Fiction* (under the pen name Kurt von Rachen) between July 1940 and February 1942. The stories open in the year 2893, after a number of attempts to overthrow the dictator who rules Earth. The government attempts to rid itself of future threats by sending rival forces to colonize a planet, hoping they will destroy each other. Among the groups are two rebels who devise means to prevent the rival groups from killing each other and whose goal is to return to Earth and overthrow the dictator. Kilkenny is a city and county in Ireland. The term *Kilkenny* *cats,* which refers to a pair of cats that legend says fought each other until only their tails remained, is used figuratively for any opponents who fight until they destroy each other. Page 140.

kill two birds: shortened version of *kill two birds with one stone,* achieve two goals with one action; accomplish two purposes by the same act or proceeding. Page 31.

kingpin: the person of chief importance in an organization, movement, undertaking, etc. Page 53.

King, Stephen: (1947–) award-winning American novelist and short-story writer and one of the world's bestselling authors. Renowned for his tales of horror, fantasy and the supernatural, King has produced many stories and books that have been made into films. Page 1.

Kline, Otis: Otis Adelbert Kline (1891–1946), American adventure writer whose novels often received serial publication in pulp magazines before release in book form. In the mid-1930s he largely abandoned writing to concentrate on a career as a literary agent. Page 78.

knack: an acquired or natural skill of doing something successfully. Page 68.

knocking around: spending time in, or traveling around, a place. Page 153.

KVOO: the group of letters (termed *call letters*) that identify a radio transmitting station, in this case one of the earliest stations in Tulsa, Oklahoma. Radio KVOO (Voice of Oklahoma) began operation in the mid-1920s, its call letters being later purchased by another station in the area. *See also* **Tulsa.** Page 61.

L

L: an *elevated* railway, a railway supported on pillars above street level. Page 70.

labor under: have a false belief; be at a disadvantage because of believing something to be true that is not. Page 89.

ladette: little lady, from *lady* plus the ending *-ette,* used for a girl and also meaning small in size. Page 96.

Ladrone: also known as the *Mariana Islands,* a Pacific island group that includes Guam. Page 109.

laid the finger on: pointed something out; indicated something. Page 68.

lambasting: criticizing (someone or something) harshly. Page 54.

last, stick to (one's): keep to that field, work, etc., in which one is competent or skilled. *To stick to one's own last* comes from an ancient story of a shoemaker criticizing a work by a Greek painter, stating that the shoe in the picture was incorrectly portrayed. Upon correction of the shoe, the shoemaker pointed out an error in the leg, upon which the painter replied, "Shoemaker, do not go above your last." A *last* is a wooden or metal form in the shape of the human foot, on which boots or shoes are shaped or repaired. Page 54.

lauded: praised highly. Page 16.

lauding: praising (of something). Page 89.

laugh, got the last: were proved right or successful in the end (after a seeming defeat or loss). Page 105.

lavatory: a room with washing and toilet facilities. Page 141.

leading light: someone who influences or sets an example to others. Page 8.

leatherneck: a slang term for a US Marine, so called from the leather lining that was part of the collar of the Marine uniform. Page 13.

leather, pull any: grab the saddle horn (a projection like a horn at the front of a horse's saddle), in reference to a rider on a bucking horse in a rodeo, who is not allowed to *pull leather* to steady himself. Page 69.

leetle: a spelling that represents a humorous pronunciation of *little,* used for emphasis. Page 155.

Left Bank: part of the city of Paris lying south of the Seine River, a famous center of artist and student life. Page 119.

Legion of Honor, Commander of the: the middle rank of five levels awarded by the Legion of Honor (a French honorary society founded by Napoleon in 1802) for outstanding achievements in military or civil life. Page 56.

Legion story: a reference to the LRH adventure story *While Bugles Blow!* about the French Foreign Legion and fighting in the desert. Published in *Five-Novels Monthly,* December 1936. Page 19.

Lesson in Lightning: an LRH story first published in *Argosy* magazine in March 1937. Though George Potts always wanted a son to match his own bravery and toughness, he ended up with small, pale, half-blind physicist Horace Potts instead. But on board a flaming Caribbean ship, Horace proves he is indeed his father's son. Page 98.

levee en masse: also spelled *levy en masse,* the drafting of large numbers of the civilian population for military service. Page 158.

level worst: a humorous variation of the expression *level best,* doing one's very best; the utmost one can possibly do. Doing one's *level worst* means doing the worst or poorest one can possibly do. Page 130.

Ley, Willy: (1906–1969) German-born writer and space advocate who helped popularize rocketry and spaceflight in Germany and the United States. Page 138.

Liberty: a weekly American magazine founded in 1924 and published through the early 1950s. It contained short stories and articles on world events. Page 9.

library card: a card issued by a library to individuals or organizations entitling them or their representatives to borrow materials. Page 69.

Library of Congress: one of the largest libraries in the world, located in Washington, DC, and housing collections totalling more than 140 million items. It was established in 1800 by the US

Congress (lawmaking body of the government) for service to its members but now also serves other government agencies, other libraries and the public. Page 55.

life, on your: said of a promise in which one would give his life before breaking the agreement, revealing a secret, etc. Page 9.

lift: a rise in condition, as in terms of state of mind, mood or the like; also, a cheering or encouraging influence or effect that contributes to such a condition. Page 15.

light love: a romantic story characterized as being *light,* not profound or serious. Page 26.

light of, by the: through the brilliance or intensity of. Page 37.

light of, make: treat as unimportant. Page 133.

literarity: the quality of being *literary,* characterized by an excessive or affected display of learning. Also, preferring books to actual experience. Page 54.

Little-Brown: the publisher Little, Brown & Company of Boston, Massachusetts, a firm founded in 1837 and noted for publishing works by many of America's finest writers. Some of their best-known titles include fiction works such as *Mutiny on the Bounty* and nonfiction such as Bartlett's *Familiar Quotations,* a work continuously updated and produced since the mid-1800s. Page 18.

little magazine: a small-format magazine, usually noncommercial, that features experimental writing or other literary expression appealing to a relatively limited number of readers. Page 56.

livestock: animals kept for use on a farm or raised for food or other products, especially farm animals such as meat and dairy cattle, pigs or the like. Page 99.

locoed: crazy, as if affected by *loco disease,* a disease that affects the nervous system, resulting in weakness, trembling and inability to move. The disease comes from having eaten *locoweed,* a plant of the pea family, found in western North America. Page 70.

loddie: a spelling that represents a humorous pronunciation of *lordy* (from *Lord*), an informal term used to express surprise, concern or annoyance about something. Page 158.

London, Jack: (1876–1916) American author, journalist, political activist and one of the most widely read American authors, with works translated into numerous languages. His adventures in gold mining and his sea voyages served as material for many of his more than fifty books. Page 63.

Lone Ranger: the name of a fictional cowboy hero of American radio, television, films, books and comics of the twentieth century. The character rode a white horse named Silver and wore a white hat and a black rectangular eye mask to conceal his true identity. He was accompanied by his faithful Indian companion, Tonto, and used silver bullets to establish law and order in the Old West. Page 130.

lone-wolfed: worked or acted on one's own in the manner of a *lone wolf,* literally, a wolf that hunts alone. Page 109.

Long, Frank Belknap: (1901–1994) American writer of horror, fantasy and science fiction stories. His works have won numerous awards throughout his career and he also is the recipient of several lifetime achievement awards. Page 145.

lookout for, on the: in the process or state of watching for (something to happen). Page 78.

look up (someone): also *look (someone) up,* locate (a person) and visit with (him). Page 55.

lost Canadian border: a reference to a 1931 United States Geological Survey team of which L. Ron Hubbard was a member. The team was to locate damaged or destroyed US/Canada border markers in the northeastern state of Maine to settle the geographic limit of the United States. Page 13.

lot, in the: in the entire group. Page 57.

lotus land: a land of ease and delight mentioned in the epic poem *Odyssey,* written by the ancient Greek poet Homer (ca. eighth century B.C.). The natives of the land were said to feed on a fruit that induced blissful forgetfulness and dreamy contentment in those who ate it. Page 114.

lowbrow: of or pertaining to a person who does not have strong or advanced intellectual interests or who lacks intellectual sophistication. Page 112.

lucre: monetary reward or gain; money. Page 114.

lurid: vivid in a harsh or shocking way; startling; sensational. Page 51.

M

Macaulay: The Macaulay Publishing Company, a publishing firm that was founded in the early 1900s, located in New York City. Page 30.

made a break: broke away; escaped. Page 70.

mad, get over your: calm down from having had a *mad,* a mood of anger about something. Page 45.

Maine: the northernmost state on the east coast of the United States. Page 13.

main track: the usual, established or widely accepted way of doing things, likened to a principal line or route of a railroad, as contrasted with a branch or secondary one. Page 95.

make light of: treat as unimportant. Page 133.

makes no never mind: an informal phrase meaning it doesn't matter, it's not important. Page 19.

maligned: spoken harmfully or untruthfully about; spoken evil of. Page 51.

mangy: having a dirty or shabby appearance. Page 96.

Man on the Flying Trapeze: a short-story collection by American writer James Thurber (1894–1961), in full *The Middle-Aged Man on the Flying Trapeze* (1935). Page 55.

"Man: The Endangered Species": the working title of *Battlefield Earth: A Saga of the Year 3000.* Page 166.

Marine (Corps): a branch of the United States armed forces trained for land, sea and air combat, typically landing near a battle zone either from the air or from a ship. Page 12.

Marines, 20th: a reserve unit of the Marine Corps. Page 16.

mark, up to the: as high as a fixed or recognized standard. Page 27.

Marquis de la Falaise de la Coudray: Henri Marquis de la Falaise de la Coudray (1898–1972), French nobleman, translator, film director, film producer and war hero. In his 1935 motion picture *Kliou the Killer,* filmed on location in the jungles of Vietnam, a young man volunteers to track down a man-eating tiger that has been terrorizing his people. Page 84.

Maryland: a state in the eastern United States on the Atlantic coast, surrounding Washington, DC, on all but one side. Page 15.

Mathieu, Hubert: Hubert "Matty" Mathieu (1897–1954), American painter, sculptor, illustrator, lecturer and writer. Mathieu created a wide variety of art and was well known for producing illustrations for magazines and newspapers, as well as for his portraits. Page 119.

matinee: a film or theatrical production presented during the day. During the 1930s many of the *film serials,* short movies shown in conjunction with a full-length film, were presented on Saturday afternoons. The series continued week after week, most with up to twelve or fifteen separate films, to draw the audience back each week for the next exciting chapter in the story. Page 24.

Matt: Hubert Mathieu (1897–1954). *See also* **Mathieu, Hubert.** Page 120.

maw: anything that seems like a gaping hole that devours things. *Maw* is literally the mouth, jaws or throat of an animal. Page 19.

McGlincy: a character in LRH's *Buckskin Brigades.* Page 129.

McIntyre, O. O.: Oscar Odd McIntyre (1884–1938), New York City newspaper columnist and critic. Page 2.

meat, (solid): matter of importance or solid substance; material that is interesting or stimulates thought. Page 61.

mebbe: an informal variation of *maybe.* Page 112.

Mein Herr: a German phrase equivalent to Sir or Mister, formerly used in addressing a man. *Mein* means my, and *Herr* means lord or master (and is used similarly to Mr. in English). Page 114.

Merchant of Venice, The: a play written in the late 1500s by English poet and dramatist William Shakespeare (1564–1616). Page 53.

MGM lot: the studios, land and facilities of *Metro-Goldwyn-Mayer,* which was one of the largest US motion picture companies. MGM was formed in the early 1900s and produced many classic films with numerous famous screen personalities. Page 26.

Mid-West: also *Middle West,* a region of the north central United States known particularly for its farmlands. Page 15.

mill: a typewriter, in reference to it as a machine for composing written copy, likened to a machine that performs certain operations on material in the process of manufacture. Used figuratively. Page 26.

mill, over the: (of the words in a story) through the typewriter (mill) and onto paper. *See also* **mill.** Page 138.

'mire: a shortened form of *quagmire,* which literally means an area of thick, slimy mud of some depth, in which one may become stuck. Used figuratively to mean a situation or state of difficulty or distress from which it is difficult to get free. Page 108.

missile: literally, any object thrown or launched as a weapon, for example, a rock or bullet. Used humorously to refer to a *missive,* a letter or written communication. Page 98.

missive: a letter or written communication. Page 7.

Missouri: 1. a state in the central United States. Page 13.

2. Missouri River, a river in the central United States; one of the largest rivers flowing into the Mississippi River, which is the largest river in the United States. Page 134.

Misterfer: a humorous variation of *Mister,* a title used in speaking or writing to a man and placed before the name. Page 112.

Mitchell, Madam: Margaret Mitchell (1900–1949), American author who wrote *Gone with the Wind.* Page 109.

monkey(ing) with: fool or mess around with (something). Page 101.

monk's cloth: a heavy cotton fabric in a basket weave (a textile weave like the checkered pattern of a woven basket), used for curtains, bedspreads, etc. Page 134.

Montana: a state in the northwestern United States bordering on Canada. Page 13.

Moore, Catherine L.: (1911–1987) an American writer of fantasy and science fiction novels and short stories. Her stories appeared in pulp magazines in the 1930s and in *Astounding Science Fiction* magazine throughout the 1940s. One of the first women to write in the genre, thus paving the way for many other female writers, Moore also was a judge for the Writers of the Future Contest from its first year. Page 61.

mos: an abbreviation for *months.* Page 156.

Moskowitz, Sam: (1920–1997) American science fiction writer, editor and science fiction anthologist. Page 145.

Mother Lode country: the region in eastern and northeastern California in the western slopes of the Sierra Nevada (a mountain range in eastern California). This region contains a *mother lode,* a term associated with the mining of gold and referring to the main deposits or layers of rich gold. The discovery of gold in this region led to the California gold rush of 1849. (A *gold rush* is a large-scale movement of people to a region where gold has been discovered.) Page 151.

Mounty: a member of the Royal Canadian Mounted Police. Page 70.

ms(s): an abbreviation for *manuscript* (and *mss,* the abbreviation for the plural), a written or typewritten text, such as one being prepared for, or awaiting, publication. Page 20.

Mudge, Prof.: Professor Mudge, the main character in LRH's *The Dangerous Dimension.* Page 126.

mum: silent and not saying a word. Page 9.

Munsey: the Frank A. Munsey Company, publisher of *Argosy* pulp magazine. Page 24.

muzzle (flash): the front open end of a gun, pistol, etc. When the gun is shot there can be a flash. Page 145.

N

name, build a: also *make a name,* create a distinguished or famous reputation. Page 26.

nary: not any. Page 165.

natural life: the period of a person's life; life span. Page 75.

Nebraska: a state in the central United States noted for its agricultural production. Page 7.

net: to obtain or achieve something. Page 7.

Never-Never Country: a reference to a line in the poem "The Explorer" by English writer Rudyard Kipling (1865–1936). The poem chronicles the trek of an explorer who, despite the warning: "There's no sense in going further—it's the edge of cultivation," ultimately discovers flourishing, uncharted lands in what doubters called the "Never-Never Country." Page 110.

Newton's laws: three laws formulated by English scientist and mathematician Sir Isaac Newton (1642–1727): (1) a body at rest remains at rest and a body in motion remains in motion unless acted on by an external force; (2) the motion of a body changes in proportion to the size of the force applied to it; (3) every action produces an equal but opposite reaction. Page 104.

new wave: any of various new or experimental trends or movements, as in literature, art or popular culture. Page 169.

Nicaraguan: of Nicaragua, the largest nation in Central America, on the Caribbean Sea and the Pacific Ocean. Formerly a Spanish colony and independent since 1838, the country has had a turbulent history with frequent intervention by foreign powers. United States Marines were stationed there between 1912 and 1933 to impose order. Page 84.

no end: to a large extent; immensely. Page 70.

Noo Yawk: also *N'Yawk,* a spelling that represents a humorous pronunciation of the name *New York,* in imitation of a New York City accent. Page 99.

north coast: the part of the Pacific coast along the Canadian province of British Columbia and north along the southern coast of Alaska. Page 119.

North Sea: the arm of the Atlantic Ocean lying between the eastern coast of Great Britain and the continent of Europe. Page 126.

not one to: not the sort of person who would (do a particular thing). Page 65.

noxious: very unpleasant or distasteful. Page 156.

NY daily: a newspaper published in New York City every weekday. Page 56.

O

officiates: performs a religious service or ceremony. Page 123.

oh-so: used as an intensive with the sense of *extremely,* usually with an ironic meaning. Page 30.

oil paper: a paper made waterproof and translucent by treatment with oil. Page 90.

oke: an informal term for *okay,* all right. Page 19.

Oklahoma: a state in the south central United States, north of the state of Texas. Page 7.

Ole Doc Methuselah: science fiction stories by LRH about the adventures of the title character, a member of the elite Soldiers of Light organization dedicated to the preservation of Mankind, combating disease, corruption and the desperate perversities of human behavior along the intergalactic spaceways. Written under the pen name of Rene LaFayette, these stories appeared in *Astounding Science Fiction* between October 1947 and January 1950. Page 155.

one-two, pulling my: a variation of *pulling one's punches,* holding something back in regard to actions, attitude, what is said, etc. From the sport of boxing, where a boxer might intentionally hold back his blows to another. (A *one-two* is a left-hand punch immediately followed by a right-hand one.) Page 109.

One Woman Alive: a mid-1930s science fiction novel by British writer Susan Ertz (1894–1985), published as a serial and later released as the novel *Woman Alive.* Page 55.

open letter: a published letter on a subject of general interest, usually addressed to an individual but intended for general readership. Page 2.

opera: another name for a written work; story. Page 149.

optics: an older term used to mean the eyes; also used humorously. Page 96.

Orders Is Orders: an LRH story first published in *Argosy* magazine in December 1937. Two Marines are assigned to brave a two-hundred mile journey, bringing desperately needed medicines across war-torn China. Page 101.

Oursler, Fulton: (1893–1952) American journalist, playwright and fiction writer. Oursler edited several American magazines, including *The Metropolitan* magazine (1923) and *Liberty* magazine (1931–1942), and wrote novels and motion picture scenarios. Page 99.

outfit: 1. a team or group of people who work closely together, such as a military unit. Page 15.

2. a large farm with its buildings, lands, etc., for the raising of cattle, horses or sheep in large numbers; ranch. Page 81.

over the mill: (of the words in a story) through the typewriter (mill) and onto paper. *See also* **mill.** Page 138.

P

Pacific Northwest: an area of the United States that includes the states of Washington, Oregon, Idaho and western Montana. Page 62.

Page, Norvell: (1904–1961) American pulp fiction writer, journalist and editor best known as the author of the majority of the adventures of the Spider, a crime fighter wanted by the law for executing his criminal antagonists. Page 136.

Paine: Thomas Paine (1737–1809), famous pamphleteer, agitator and writer on politics and religion whose works influenced political thinking at the time of the Revolutionary War in America (1775–1783). Page 104.

palsy: a physical condition of muscular inability to move part or all of the body, sometimes accompanied by involuntary trembling of the limbs. Page 36.

panning: washing (gravel, for example) in a pan to separate out gold or other precious metal. Page 157.

pard: a shortened form of *pardner*. *See also* **pardner.** Page 158.

pardner: a humorous pronunciation of *partner,* a companion or friend. Page 112.

par excellence: in the greatest degree of excellence; beyond comparison. Page 24.

parting shot: a last statement or action taken before parting (leaving a place, subject, etc.). Page 57.

Pasadena: a city in southwest California, near Los Angeles. Page 147.

past master: somebody with great experience and skill (in doing something). Page 37.

pastures, greener: a place or activity regarded as offering new opportunities. Page 79.

patent(s): 1. an exclusive right officially granted by a government to an inventor to produce, use or sell an invention. Page 91.

2. covered with *patent leather,* leather with a smooth, glossy surface. Page 151.

pave the road: prepare the way. Page 147.

Peiping: also spelled *Peking,* former name of Beijing, capital of China, located in the northeastern part of the country. Page 15.

Penna: an abbreviation for *Pennsylvania,* a state in the eastern United States. Page 124.

penned: written with or as if with a pen. Page 7.

pensively: in a manner characterized by deep thought about something, especially in a sad or serious way. Page 112.

pent: confined or restrained; not released. Page 109.

perennially: in a way that endures; constantly or permanently. Page 1.

perforce: by necessity; by force of circumstance. Page 34.

perusal: a reading through or over (of something). Page 41.

Pestilence: literally, an epidemic of a highly contagious fatal disease, such as the plague, that kills many people. Used here in reference to the Biblical description of the evils that will come at the end of the world, symbolized by the Four Horsemen who ride white, red, black and pale horses, symbolizing pestilence, war, famine and death, respectively. Page 107.

"Phantasmagoria": the LRH story published as *Fear* in *Unknown* magazine, July 1940. *Phantasmagoria* means a constantly shifting, complex succession of things seen or imagined (as in a dream or state of fever). Page 131.

Philtower: short for *Philtower Building,* a twenty-four-story building and landmark in Tulsa, Oklahoma, in the south central United States. Financed by a renowned local oilman (Waite Phillips), the building was completed in 1928 and was home to the radio station KVOO. Page 80.

phobia: a very powerful fear and dislike of something. Page 26.

piano accordion: also *accordion,* a portable wind instrument having a large bellows (a device for producing a strong current of air by expanding and contracting) that forces air through small metal reeds, a keyboard for the right hand and buttons for playing single notes with the left hand. Page 136.

Pierce, Frank: Frank Richardson Pierce, a writer for pulp magazines, who contributed stories to such well-known publications as *Argosy* and *Western Story.* Page 22.

Pinkerton: *Pinkerton National Detective Agency,* one of the first private detective agencies in the United States, founded in 1850 by Allan Pinkerton (1819–1884). Page 84.

pious: deserving to be praised; commendable. Page 47.

pip: an excellent or admirable person or thing. Short for *pippin,* a type of apple valued as a dessert. Page 103.

pirated: published, reproduced or made use of without authorization, such as a literary work, music or the like. Page 78.

pistol: literally, a small gun that is held in, and fired from, one hand. Used humorously to refer to an *epistle,* a formal term for a letter, especially a long, formal, instructive letter. Page 96.

play: a show of interest, attention or support. Page 148.

play a hand with: become involved in an activity with another. From playing cards, where a *hand* is the cards dealt to each player at the beginning of a card game or a round of play with these cards. Page 85.

Plot Genie: a device developed in the early 1900s and used by some writers to develop plots for their stories. The Plot Genie consists of a disk with 180 numbers, with a slot allowing only one number to be seen at a time. The author turns the disk and randomly selects a number, which shows in the slot. The number refers to one of several plot elements, such as locale, male character, female character, problem, obstacle, etc. He then refers to a list containing the various choices assigned to each number and copies from the list the specific element the number refers to. The writer then takes these random elements and incorporates them into his story. Page 107.

plugging: working steadily at something. Page 62.

Poe: Edgar Allan Poe (1809–1849), American short story writer, poet and journalist. His tales of mystery and horror have been reprinted over and over again. Many of his works, especially his poems, express extreme sadness and depression. Page 129.

poorhouse: a place maintained at public expense to house needy or dependent persons. Page 147.

Popular (Publications): one of the largest publishers of pulp magazines, with titles covering western fiction, romance, detective and adventure. Page 54.

Port Orchard: a resort and fishing community located in western Washington State on *Puget Sound,* a long, narrow bay of the Pacific Ocean on the northwestern coast of the United States. Page 7.

Post: A. Worthington Post, associate editor of *Argosy* magazine. Page 141.

power flight: the activity of flying aircraft that receive power from a motor using electrical energy or fuel such as gasoline. Page 15.

Pratt, Fletcher: Murray Fletcher Pratt (1897–1956), American writer of science fiction, fantasy and naval history, particularly on the American Civil War. Page 136.

precinct: the police unit or station situated in an area of a city or town. Page 86.

preempted: taken for oneself to the exclusion of others. Page 41.

press: pressure in one's work or other activities. Page 22.

pretty, sitting: is in a fortunate or advantageous position. Page 26.

process: in law, an action or suit. Page 91.

proclivities: natural or habitual inclinations or tendencies. Page 89.

promise: an indication that something is likely to develop successfully. Page 34.

pseudo-: a word combined with other words to mean false or pretended. Also apparently similar to (a specified thing) as in pseudo-scientist, pseudo-ally. Page 11.

public enemy: a person or thing considered a danger or menace to the public, especially a wanted criminal in the US widely sought by the FBI (Federal Bureau of Investigation) and local police forces. Page 68.

Puerto Rican mining expedition: also known as the *West Indies Mineralogical Expedition,* an expedition organized and conducted by L. Ron Hubbard during the early 1930s. The expedition also toured other Caribbean islands while conducting its primary mission, the first complete mineralogical survey of Puerto Rico under United States jurisdiction. Page 7.

puhhaps: a spelling that represents a humorous pronunciation of *perhaps*. Page 129.

pulling my one-two: a variation of *pulling one's punches,* holding something back in regard to actions, attitude, what is said, etc. From the sport of boxing, where a boxer might intentionally hold back his blows to another. (A *one-two* is a left-hand punch immediately followed by a right-hand one.) Page 109.

pulling punches: holding something back in regard to actions, attitude, what is said, etc. The phrase *pulling one's punches* comes from boxing, where a boxer might intentionally hold back his blows to another. Page 110.

pulpateer: a writer for the pulps, from the word *pulp* combined with the ending *-ateer,* a variation of *-eer,* a person who produces, handles or is otherwise significantly associated with (the pulps). Page 51.

puncher: a shortened form of *cowpuncher,* an informal term for a cowboy. In this term, *punch* means jab or poke cattle in herding. Page 55.

punch the clock: literally, put a time card in the time clock for noting time of arrival and departure. A *time clock* is a clock with an attachment that may be manually activated to punch or stamp the exact time on a card or tape, used to keep a record of the time of something, as of the arrival and departure of employees. Page 53.

punk: poor in quality. Page 103.

pursuit pilot(s): a reference to someone who flies a *pursuit plane,* a fast and highly maneuverable airplane that may be equipped with bombs, rockets, etc., for fighting enemy aircraft. Page 68.

put up: engaged in or carried on, as a fight. Page 34.

pyrites: a shiny compound of iron and sulfur. Pyrites are found in many places, are often mistaken for gold and sometimes are called "fool's gold." The name *pyrite* comes from the Greek word for fire. Page 157.

Q

Quantico: a United States Marine Corps base founded in 1917 and located in Quantico, Virginia, about 35 miles (56 kilometers) south of Washington, DC. It is the chief location for training officers of the United States Marine Corps. Page 16.

quart(s): a unit of liquid capacity equal to a quarter of a gallon, or two pints, equivalent to approximately 0.94 liter. Page 13.

quartz, honey-comb: *quartz,* a brilliant, crystalline mineral, often found in conjunction with gold. Some forms of quartz appear as crystals in which each crystal has six sides, like the individual cells of a honey-comb (a wax structure made by bees to store honey and eggs). Page 15.

quill pen-blue-slip regiments: large numbers of persons (regiments) who write rejection slips (blue slips) using quill pens. A *quill pen* is an old-fashioned pen made from the shaft of a feather, with its split and sharpened end dipped in ink. Page 156.

R

rabble: those regarded as the common, low, disorderly part of the populace. Page 158.

racy: full of energy or spirit. Page 32.

rampage, on the: rushing around in a reckless way; in a state of being turbulently active or wildly agitated. Page 109.

Ranch Romances: one of the longest-running pulp magazines, *Ranch Romances* began in the 1920s and was published until the early 1970s. Page 8.

rate: estimate the value or worth of; rank. Page 54.

rattler: a slang term for a railway train. Page 71.

razz(ed): tease; make fun of. Page 96.

reaching: having a strong effect; influencing or affecting. Page 153.

Realpolitick: a German word meaning *practical politics,* politics based on practical considerations, such as the realities of national interest and power, especially as distinguished from theoretical, ethical or moralistic objectives. Page 157.

rear-guard, riding: literally, proceeding as the *rear-guard,* the part of a military force that is stationed behind the main body to protect the rear from surprise attack. Used figuratively for any similar actions of following and protecting those ahead. Page 107.

Reconstruction: the process of reorganizing the Southern states back into the United States of America after the Civil War, the conflict between the North and the South (1861–1865) that occurred primarily over the issue of slavery, which was abolished as a result of the war. During Reconstruction, racism, harsh measures and injustices prompted an extreme reaction from many white Southerners, who in turn forced newly freed blacks into a second-class status that lasted until well into the twentieth century. Page 158.

red flag: something that indicates danger or trouble ahead and consequently advises a slowing down or stopping of action. Page 20.

red scare: a time or condition of alarm or worry about *reds,* those who support communism. Used in reference to O. O. McIntyre's remarks about writers in America spreading communist propaganda. Page 54.

regiments, quill pen-blue-slip: large numbers of persons (regiments) who write rejection slips (blue slips) using quill pens. A *quill pen* is an old-fashioned pen made from the shaft of a feather, with its split and sharpened end dipped in ink. Page 156.

remark (something): notice or observe (something). Page 56.

Remington: a typewriter manufactured by the Remington & Sons company of New York City. Remington typewriters were first produced in the early 1870s. Page 26.

renegades: people who choose to live outside laws or conventions; rebels. Page 18.

rep: short for *reputation.* Page 9.

retail: repeat or tell again in detail. Page 98.

retreat: a place of refuge, seclusion or privacy. Page 22.

rhumba band: a group of musicians who perform music for dancing the *rhumba,* a rhythmically complex dance of Cuban origin. Page 136.

ribbing: playful or friendly teasing. Page 42.

ribbon: a band of inked material, used in a typewriter, that supplies ink for printing the figure on the striking typeface onto the paper beneath. Page 33.

right, do (the place): visit and explore (a place) as or as if a sightseer or tourist to the most complete extent or degree. Page 71.

right of, to the: even more extreme in right-wing activities or beliefs. *Right* refers to conservative political systems and views in favor of preserving traditional values and customs and against abrupt change. Extreme right-wing systems include fascism, where a group or nation is led by a dictator having complete power, forcibly suppressing opposition and criticism and emphasizing an aggressive nationalism (excessive or fanatical devotion to a nation and its interests, often associated with a belief that one country is superior to all others). Page 51.

right wing: of or relating to the conservative membership of a group or political party. Page 158.

Rip: Rip Van Winkle, the main character in a story of the same name by Washington Irving. Rip falls asleep for twenty years and, upon waking, is startled to find how much the world has changed. Page 108.

Ritz: giving an appearance of being very stylish or expensive, from the name of the elegant hotels created by Swiss hotel manager César Ritz (1850–1918). Page 156.

Riverside Drive: a famous street in New York City, overlooking the Hudson River. The street is known for its impressive buildings, monuments and fine parks, as well as being a fashionable residential area. Page 11.

Roan, Tom: pen name of Thomas Rowan (1894?–1958), a prolific writer of the 1920s through the 1950s. He wrote numerous western stories for the pulps as well as several western novels. Page 68.

Robespierre: the French lawyer and revolutionary leader Maximilien Robespierre (1758–1794), who helped bring about the *Reign of Terror,* a period in which thousands of suspected opponents of the French Revolution were executed. Page 158.

Rockefeller Center: a large group of buildings in the heart of New York City, built by American businessman John D. Rockefeller, Jr. (1874–1960). The original fourteen buildings were constructed between 1930 and 1933, with several more buildings added over the years. The Rockefeller Center ice-skating facility opened on Christmas Day, 1936, prominently located in the sunken plaza in the middle of the complex, and rapidly became one of the most popular spots in the city for winter activities. Page 136.

rococo: ornamentation or detail, as in writing, that is intricate or elaborate. Page 77.

roll: 1. a list of names of persons belonging to a given group. Page 15.

2. a slang term for money, especially a wad of paper money. Page 71.

roll(ing)(ed): produce or form (something) as if by passing a material between rollers, such as those on a typewriter. Page 24.

Romeo Reverse: a novel written in 1934 by Edward Dean Sullivan (1888–1938), a parody of *Anthony Adverse,* a popular historical novel (1933) and film. *See also* **Scurvy Gallon.** Page 109.

romp home: run or move swiftly in a race or contest so as to win easily, used figuratively and ironically. Page 101.

Roosevelt: Franklin D. Roosevelt (1882–1945), thirty-second president of the United States (1933–1945). He was the only president elected four times. Roosevelt led the United States through the economic depression of the 1930s and through World War II (1939–1945). Page 20.

ropes, knowing the: knowing how and becoming familiar with a particular job or task, the customary actions or practices of some area, field, etc. It comes from the days of sailing ships, where a sailor became thoroughly familiar with handling the ropes and equipment for raising and lowering the sails on a ship. Page 73.

rotary system, helicopter: the mechanism that enables the rotating (turning) blade of a helicopter to move. Page 95.

rough-stock periodical: a magazine printed on paper (stock) that has a rough surface, usually making it less expensive than smooth-surfaced paper. Page 1.

roulette, dish: *roulette* is a gambling game in which a small ball is rolled onto a spinning horizontal wheel. The wheel is curved inward, like a dish, and is divided into numbered compartments. Players bet on which compartment the ball will come to rest in. *Dish* means serve something by placing it into a dish and here is used figuratively with reference to rolling the small ball onto the roulette wheel. Hence *dish roulette,* play the gambling game of roulette. Page 96.

rounds, going the: going around from place to place, as in a habitual or definite circuit or route. Page 54.

royalty: an agreed portion of the income from a work, paid to its author, composer, etc., by a publisher, etc., usually a percentage of the price of each copy sold. Page 65.

Rt.: an abbreviation for *route,* a road or highway. Page 22.

run(ning) down: criticize severely. Page 56.

running, out of the: no longer in the competition; no longer having a chance to win. Page 26.

runt: an offensive term for somebody regarded as short in height or lacking physical strength. Page 42.

S

Sabotage in the Sky: an LRH story first published in *Five-Novels Monthly* magazine in August 1940. Airborne in one of the hottest fighter planes being tested, pilot Bill Trevillian finds that someone has deliberately rigged the aircraft for failure and destruction—and for Trevillian's death. Page 140.

salt horse: salted meat (as beef or pork). Page 13.

sample pick: a type of lightweight, hand-held pick used by prospectors and miners in taking samples, often having a square head on one end for hammering into surfaces and a pointed tip on the other end for breaking up ore. Taking samples involves striking off bits of rock along a rock face, collecting the bits and then having them analyzed to determine their mineral content. Page 15.

S&S: an abbreviation for the publishing company Street & Smith. *See also* **Street & Smith.** Page 96.

Satevepost: *Saturday Evening Post,* a general magazine featuring text and photographs on a wide range of subjects. The magazine was published weekly from 1821 to 1969. It went out of business in 1969 but was revived as a monthly publication in 1971. Page 114.

satire: the use of humor, irony, exaggeration or ridicule to expose and criticize people's stupidity or vices. Page 129.

Sayer: Walter William Sayer (1892–1982), a writer for the pulps in the 1920s–1930s under the pen name of Pierre Quiroule. Page 68.

scenario: an outline of a motion picture, giving the action in the order in which it takes place, the description of scenes and characters, etc. Page 78.

schooner: a sailing ship with sails set lengthwise (fore and aft) and having from two to as many as seven masts. Page 13.

Scientology: Scientology is the study and handling of the spirit in relationship to itself, universes and other life. The term Scientology is taken from the Latin *scio,* which means "knowing in the fullest sense of the word" and the Greek word *logos,* meaning "study of." In itself the word means literally "knowing how to know." Page 1.

Scott: Sir Walter Scott (1771–1832), Scottish novelist, poet and critic, one of the most prominent and influential figures in English literature, especially famous for his historical novels. In *Ivanhoe* he presented cultural conflicts in England of the early Middle Ages and in a popular series called the Waverly novels, which included *Rob Roy* and five other books, he portrayed key events in Scottish history. Page 56.

scrap: struggle or fight. Page 109.

script doctor: one who revises or alters a script to improve it. Page 24.

scud cloud: low-drifting clouds appearing beneath a cloud from which precipitation is falling. Page 120.

Scurvy Gallon: a made-up name, a play on the name Hervey Allen (1889–1949), American author, best known for his historical novel *Anthony Adverse* (1933). Page 109.

second officer: the officer of a merchant vessel next in command beneath the first mate, who is directly below the captain. Also called *second mate.* Page 107.

Secret of Treasure Island, The: the series of films produced by Columbia Pictures, drawn from the L. Ron Hubbard novel *Murder at Pirate Castle.* LRH's screenplays for the serial, written during 1937, became a box office success. Page 7.

Seine: a river in France, flowing northwest through Paris to the English Channel, 480 miles (773 kilometers) long. Page 119.

Semper Fidelis: a Latin phrase meaning always faithful, the motto of the US Marine Corps. Page 15.

señor: a Spanish title equivalent to English "Mr." Page 26.

serial: 1. a motion picture presented in a number of successive installments. Page 24.
2. a story that is published in parts, normally at regular intervals. Page 31.

serially: in the form of a *serial,* a story that is published in parts, normally at regular intervals. Page 55.

service background: a history of employment in a branch of military service. Page 2.

service station: a place that provides maintenance service, parts, supplies, gasoline and oil, etc., for motor vehicles. Page 62.

servile: very eager to obey someone in order to please them. Page 36.

setup: the organization, arrangements or equipment necessary for a particular activity. Page 112.

77 Sunset Strip: a popular television program that ran from 1958 to 1964, focusing on private detectives in Los Angeles, California. One of the most influential of the private-eye shows, the name *77 Sunset Strip* reflected a fictional address on the famous *Sunset Strip,* the section of Sunset Boulevard renowned for its nightlife and celebrities. Page 79.

s/f: an abbreviation for *science fiction.* Page 156.

shade: a little bit; slightly. Page 101.

Shakespeare: William Shakespeare (1564–1616), English poet and dramatist; the most widely known author in all English literature. Page 56.

Shanghai: a seaport and the largest city in China, located on the eastern coast of the country. Shanghai is a center of industry, trade and finance. Page 15.

shapes up: evolves or develops. Page 35.

Shasta Pub: a publishing company in Chicago, Illinois, that operated between 1947 and 1957. Shasta specialized in science fiction and fantasy publications. Page 156.

shelf life: the period of time during which a book is popular and considered saleable. Page 30.

shiftless: lazy and lacking determination or a firm purpose. Page 112.

Shin-ho: a designation for the city of Shanghai, from Shen and Hu, traditional nicknames for the city. *Shen* was a ruler in ancient times (yet another nickname for the city being *Shencheng,* the City of Shen), while *hu* is an early fishing tool used in the area. Page 15.

sho: a spelling that represents an informal pronunciation of *sure,* used here to emphasize what is being said. Page 141.

shoot along: hand over or send forward quickly to someone or to a destination. Page 11.

shooting these arrows into the air: a reference to the poem "The Arrow and the Song" (1845) by American writer Henry Wadsworth Longfellow (1807–1882). The poem compares an arrow with a song: both are sent out and land somewhere, one knows not where. The poem ends:
> *"Long, long afterward, in an oak*
> *I found the arrow, still unbroke;*
> *And the song, from beginning to end,*
> *I found again in the heart of a friend."* Page 35.

shore: a spelling that represents a humorous pronunciation of *sure*. Page 158.

short: a *short story,* a work of fiction that differs from a novel by being shorter and less elaborate. Page 45.

shove off: depart; go away. Literally, push a boat away from the shore when leaving. Page 71.

shrapnel: metal balls or fragments that are scattered when a shell, bomb or bullet explodes. Page 145.

shucks: *shucks* refers to something of little or no value. *Not* (doing something) *worth shucks* means not doing something well. Page 159.

Si: short for *Silas,* a man's name, here humorously representing an old-fashioned type of name, like one that might be used in a rural area. Page 96.

sicced: figuratively, urged someone to do something. From the literal sense of *sic,* urge a person or animal, especially a dog, to attack somebody physically. Page 26.

sidling up to: moving or walking toward someone in a manner intended to escape notice. Page 56.

sinceripatedly: representing an informal pronunciation and play on the word *sincerely*. Page 113.

six-gun: a handgun from which six shots can be fired without reloading. This type of gun was used frequently during the American Civil War (1861–1865) and in the pioneer days of the American West. Page 82.

Six-Gun Caballero: an LRH story first published in *Western Story* magazine in March 1938. Michael Patrick Obañon, proud owner of a 100,000-acre ranch willed to him by his father, stands to lose his entire inheritance when a band of criminals makes false claims on his property. Page 82.

sizzled: figuratively, burned with scorching heat, typically so as to produce a hissing sound, as if from resentment or anger. Page 110.

skipper: the captain of a ship. Page 145.

skoal: to your health (used as a drinking toast). Page 82.

skunk cabbage: a plant of the swampy areas of North America, known for its unpleasant, skunklike odor. The leaves of the skunk cabbage are broad and 1 to 3 feet (30 to 91 centimeters) long. Page 95.

Sky Birds Dare!: an LRH story first published in *Five-Novels Monthly* magazine in September 1936. The world of gliders comes to life in this story of a glider pilot, his determination to prove the worth of gliders and the ruthless competitor who is trying to destroy him. Page 18.

sky-rocket: a rocket firework that ascends into the air and explodes at a height, usually in a brilliant display of sparks of one or more colors. Used figuratively. Page 109.

slam-bang (up) against: intensely or deeply involved in (something) as if forcefully slammed against it. Page 36.

slant: point of view; angle; direction (toward a particular subject or public). Page 70.

slate, clear: a schedule that has had engagements, appointments or the like removed or completed. Page 22.

Slaves of Sleep: an LRH story first published in *Unknown* magazine in July 1939. Jan Palmer witnesses the murder of Professor Frobish by Zongri, an angry demon that the professor had freed from a copper jar. Cursed by the demon with eternal wakefulness, Jan ends up not only jailed for murder, but also struggling to free himself from a nightmare world ruled by the demon. Page 129.

sleeves, rolled up (one's): prepared for action. The expression comes from the action of *rolling up* one's shirt *sleeves* just before doing work, to prevent them from getting dirty and to allow greater freedom of movement to the arms. Page 33.

slick(s): also *slick paper,* a magazine printed on paper having a more or less glossy finish and regarded as possessing such qualities as expensiveness and sophistication. Page 56.

slipstick: a device for making precise mathematical calculations, such as multiplication and division, consisting of a ruler with a sliding piece. Also called a *slide rule.* Page 13.

Sloane, Bill: William M. Sloane (1906–1974), American author of fantasy and science fiction. He formed his own publishing company, William Sloane Associates, in 1946. Page 152.

slush pile: a collection of manuscripts sent to a publisher without being requested. Page 7.

smacking of: being strongly suggestive of or a reminder of. Page 7.

small hours: the early morning hours after midnight. Page 138.

Snake River: a river of the northwestern United States, approximately 1,040 miles (1,670 kilometers) long. The Snake River begins in Wyoming and flows westward through Idaho and Washington State. Page 33.

sneaking: gradually growing or persistent, as in a *sneaking hunch*. A *hunch* is a feeling or guess that something will happen or may be the case. Page 91.

soaring plane: a motorless plane that uses upward air currents to stay aloft, often soaring for several hours at a time. Such aircraft are usually towed to the correct altitude by another aircraft, as an airplane, or by an automobile. Page 15.

sojourned: stayed temporarily. Page 74.

soldier of fortune: someone who will join any army as a soldier so that he can find profit or adventure. Page 11.

son-of-a-gun: an informal phrase for a fellow, character, guy or individual. Page 35.

SoundScriber: the brand name of a machine produced from the late 1940s to the mid-1960s that recorded voice on small discs for transcription. SoundScriber discs were noted for their compact size, which allowed them to be mailed. Page 145.

sour: destroy the faith or enthusiasm of; disappoint. Page 9.

sour grapes: complaints, disdain; contempt. A reference to the fable wherein a fox, after futile efforts to reach some grapes, scorns them as being sour. Page 109.

spasm(s): a sudden violent and temporary activity, effort or emotion. Page 82.

speculative: of writing that is usually considered to include fantasy, horror, science fiction and the like, dealing with worlds unlike the real world. Page 1.

spill the beans: reveal secret information. Page 9.

Spinoza: Benedict Spinoza (1632–1677), Dutch philosopher and religious thinker. He believed that Man's highest happiness consists in coming to understand and appreciate the truth that he is a tiny part of a god who is present in everything. Page 104.

spoofing: joking or fooling (about something). Page 158.

Sportsman Pilot: a monthly American aviation magazine published from around 1930 until 1943. It contained writings on a wide range of subjects, including coverage of aerial sporting events, commentary on current aviation issues, technical articles on flying as well as other articles on topics of general interest. Page 98.

Sprague: L. Sprague de Camp (1907–2000), American writer who produced works of fantasy, nonfiction, fiction and science fiction during a sixty-year literary career. Page 136.

"Springfield Mountain": an early American ballad based on a true story of a young man who died from a rattlesnake bite in 1761 in Springfield Mountain, Massachusetts, in the northeastern United States. Page 90.

squads east and west: a reference to military commands shouted to a squad (the smallest military unit of soldiers, commonly consisting of twelve soldiers), commanding a turn to the east or a turn to the west. Page 15.

Squad That Never Came Back, The: an LRH story first published in *Thrilling Adventures* magazine in May 1935. Threatened with death, a corporal leads a group of fellow legionnaires to a lost treasure in the Moroccan desert. Originally written by LRH under the pen name Kurt von Rachen, it was published under the pen name Legionnaire 148. Page 8.

squint: a look or glance, often casual. Page 101.

stable(s): a group or staff of writers engaged to contribute their services when called upon; pool. Page 7.

stale: without freshness. Page 66.

stamp out: suppress or crush. Page 56.

Standard Magazines: a publishing company that produced a number of well-known pulp magazines, such as *Thrilling Adventures, Thrilling Detective, Thrilling Western, Startling Stories* and others. Operating from the 1930s to the early 1960s, the company was also called Thrilling Publications, Beacon Magazines and Better Publications. Page 7.

stands, on the: displayed for sale on *newsstands,* small booths on the street, from which newspapers, magazines and books are sold to passersby. Something *on the stands* has been placed in the newsstands and become available for the public to buy. Page 56.

Startling (Stories): a science fiction magazine published by Standard Magazines. Page 150.

static search party: a group of people searching for the source of static electricity (which, in the context, was coming from an electric typewriter) in order to handle electrical interference interrupting a nearby radio broadcast. Page 141.

station house: a building housing a police department. Page 85.

steeplejack: a skilled construction worker who performs installations, maintenance and repairs on skyscrapers, towers, steeples, smokestacks and other tall structures. Page 69.

Stetson: a type of felt hat with a broad brim and a high crown, particularly popular in the Western US. Named after John B. Stetson (1830–1906), who originated it in the mid-1800s. Page 13.

STI: an abbreviation for LRH's *The Secret of Treasure Island. See also* **Secret of Treasure Island, The.** Page 24.

stick to (one's) last: keep to that field, work, etc., in which one is competent or skilled. *To stick to one's own last* comes from an ancient story of a shoemaker criticizing a work by a Greek painter, stating that the shoe in the picture was incorrectly portrayed. Upon correction of the shoe, the shoemaker pointed out an error in the leg, upon which the painter replied, "Shoemaker, do not go above your last." A *last* is a wooden or metal form in the shape of the human foot, on which boots or shoes are shaped or repaired. Page 54.

stint: a period of time spent doing something. Page 7.

stock: describing something as typical, familiar and therefore lacking in originality; from the idea of a supply of items (stock) used so frequently that they are kept available on a regular basis. Page 51.

stoking: feeding abundantly or providing more than adequately with food. Page 89.

storm the heights: attack and capture a high place, especially a well-defended one, suddenly and with great force. Page 16.

St. Pete: informal for St. Peter, who is traditionally the gatekeeper of Heaven. Page 15.

strays: a figurative reference to stories not purchased or published elsewhere. A *stray* is a person or domestic animal without a home. Page 28.

stream-bucking: forcing one's way through or proceeding against an obstacle. Literally, going upstream against the force of water flowing in the opposite direction. Page 104.

stream of consciousness: an individual's thoughts and conscious reaction to external events experienced subjectively as a continuous flow. Page 43.

Street & Smith: a large American publishing company established in the mid-1800s that put out a large number of periodicals and pulp magazines in the late nineteenth and early twentieth centuries, such as *Astounding Science Fiction* magazine and *Unknown* magazine. Page 40.

string of (something): a continuous series or succession (of something, such as songs, stories, questions, incidents or the like). Page 53.

stroke counter: a device on a typewriter that counts up the *strokes,* the times that a key on the keyboard is pressed down, and keeps a total of the number of strokes. Page 114.

strokes, broader: literally, a wide mark of a pen or pencil when writing or a brush when painting. Hence, *broader strokes,* a more general view or picture of a topic or subject. Page 1.

strongman: a person who performs remarkable feats of strength, as in a circus. Page 45.

Stroudsburg: a city in northern Pennsylvania, a state in the eastern United States, about 80 miles (125 kilometers) north of Philadelphia. Page 149.

Strudemeyer, Dallas: a proposed pen name for LRH. Page 156.

sub-child: characterized as being at a lower level or position than a child, as in intelligence, interest or the like. Page 89.

sullenly: in a manner expressing gloomy or resentful silence. Page 108.

surmised: concluded or supposed that something was possible or likely. Page 155.

swamping out: clearing out underbrush or cutting down trees. From the logging industry, where swamping out is done to make a rough road, as for hauling trees out of the forest. Page 114.

swamps: 1. floods or drenches with water or the like. Page 141.

2. (of a business) fails or becomes ruined financially, likened to a boat that becomes filled with water and sinks. Page 156.

swell: an informal term meaning excellent or very good. Page 56.

swing: a style of jazz or dance music with an easy-flowing but vigorous rhythm. Page 141.

swing, into: operating at a high speed or level of activity; into operation. Page 147.

syllables, long line of: many words or stories. A *syllable* is a unit of pronunciation; a word or part of a word pronounced with a single, uninterrupted sounding of the voice. Page 20.

T

taboos: also *tabus,* prohibitions or restrictions of the use or practice of something considered improper or unacceptable. Page 11.

tag: a popular description, label, nickname or the like. Page 153.

tagging: an informal term meaning following closely. Page 81.

tall starving: considerable starving. *Tall* in this context means large in amount or degree. Page 63.

Tarangpang: an unpublished work written by L. Ron Hubbard, about a US Army engineer in the Philippines who becomes a skilled diplomat when a reckless killing angers the local people. Page 129.

tarheel: a syrup made of molasses and maple syrup. Page 13.

tch: a representation of the click made by pressing some part of the tongue against the roof of the mouth and then pulling it away quickly. Used here humorously, as if in expressing mild annoyance. Page 96.

techno-minded: interested in or inclined to things that involve the subjects of science and technology. Page 40.

tekneekew: a spelling that represents a humorous pronunciation of *technique.* Page 158.

teleplay: a treatment or script for a play written for presentation on television. Page 61.

Terrill, Rog: Rogers Terrill, editor at *Popular Publications,* one of the largest publishers of pulp magazines during the first half of the twentieth century. Page 148.

Things to Come: a novel (in full, *The Shape of Things to Come*) written in 1933 by H. G. Wells (1866–1946). Page 55.

threshed: talked over thoroughly and vigorously in order to reach a decision, conclusion or understanding; discussed exhaustively. Page 123.

thumbnail sketch: a short, usually descriptive, essay, history or story. Page 7.

thumbs, all: lacking physical coordination, skill or grace; clumsy or awkward, as if one's hands contained all thumbs and no fingers. Page 124.

thunk: a humorous use of a past form of *think*. Page 114.

tickles: makes (someone) pleased. Page 169.

tie into: get to work on vigorously. Page 27.

tie-up: 1. a halting of something. Page 20.
2. an informal term meaning something that is connected or related. Used figuratively to mean making two things coincide or happen at the same time. Page 80.

tiffin: a light midday meal or snack. Used figuratively. Page 82.

Timbuktu: a city in central Mali, a country in northwestern Africa on the southern edge of the Sahara Desert. Founded in the late eleventh century A.D., Timbuktu became a center of Islamic learning. The name of this city is often used in phrases to represent a place that is very far away. Page 13.

time, did: spent a period of time in jail. Page 82.

Tinhorn's Daughter: an LRH story first published in *Western Romances* magazine in December 1937. A tale about a girl whose sweetheart—gallant, red-haired Sunset Maloney—has sworn to shoot it out with her tinhorn fraud of a father. (A *tinhorn* is someone, especially a gambler, who pretends to be important but actually has little money, influence or skill.) Page 103.

tinker-toy: characteristic of or similar to *Tinkertoy,* a brand name for a construction toy consisting of wooden pieces such as rods and wheels that can be fitted together to assemble structures and other things. Page 129.

Tin Pan Alley: a district of New York City, where there are many songwriters, publishers of popular music, etc. In the early 1900s, musicians' slang included the phrase *tin pan* for a cheap piano with a tinny (thin and metallic) sound. Since those were the pianos associated with the music publishing district of New York, the area became known as *Tin Pan Alley*. Page 88.

tip-off: special and useful information given as a piece of advice. Page 105.

tish: a variation of *tush,* an expression used here humorously to show mild disapproval. Page 96.

titleer, prize: the best (prize) person in coming up with good titles for articles, stories, etc. *Titleer* is a made-up word, from *title* and the ending *-eer,* for a person who produces, handles or is otherwise significantly associated with (titles). Page 20.

toes, turns up its: dies, in reference to the position in which a body is placed for burial, with the toes pointing up. Page 108.

top-kicker: a military slang term for a top sergeant. Hence *top-kicker in the 20th,* top sergeant in the 20th Marines, a reserve unit of the Marine Corps. *See also* **top sergeant.** Page 15.

top-line: of the highest reputation, quality or importance. From the literal meaning of *top line,* so important as to be named at or near the top of a newspaper item, advertisement or the like. Page 7.

top-notch: first-rate or excellent. Page 42.

top-notchers: the highest professionals in a field. Page 83.

top sergeant: a *first sergeant,* a lower-ranked officer of the US Army or Marines, particularly one serving as chief administrative assistant to the commander of a group of soldiers. Page 95.

toss off: do something quickly and easily. Page 45.

touching: in reference or relation to; concerning; about. Page 85.

tow: pull something such as a trailer behind one's car. Hence *"tow south,"* pull a trailer and head toward the south. Page 151.

to wit: used to introduce a list or explanation of what one has just mentioned. Originally a phrase used in law, *that is to wit,* which meant that is to know, that is to say. Page 145.

track, main: the usual, established or widely accepted way of doing things, likened to a principal line or route of a railroad, as contrasted with a branch or secondary one. Page 95.

transit: an instrument with a telescope on top, employed in measuring land and in calculating angles and lengths. Page 13.

transport plane: an aircraft used for transporting troops, supplies, etc. Page 54.

trek out: make a long, difficult journey. Page 71.

tricked up: dressed up or made to appear a certain way, likened to decorating something. Page 146.

trimmings, with the: with additional things, such as the items of food traditionally served as accompaniments to a main dish. Page 134.

trim, out of: *trim* means fitness, especially a suitable or excellent condition for a particular task or for general action. It also refers to the condition or state of readiness (of someone or something) for work or action of any kind. Thus to be *out of trim* means to be out of shape and not ready for work or action. Page 62.

tripe: something worthless; nonsense. Page 57.

truck: dealings. Page 112.

Tsingtao: also spelled *Qingdao,* a port city, naval base and industrial center at the entrance to *Jiaozhou Bay,* a sheltered harbor in northeastern China. The city and surrounding areas were occupied by the Japanese between 1914 and 1922, and again during World War II (1939–1945). Page 105.

Tulsa: a city in northeastern Oklahoma, a state in the south central United States. Page 83.

Tumon: a beach area, now a resort, on the west coast of the island of Guam. Page 14.

turn(ed) out: produce or create something, especially in a consistent way with rapidity or skill. Page 20.

turns, by: one thing following after another. Page 7.

turns up its toes: dies, in reference to the position in which a body is placed for burial, with the toes pointing up. Page 108.

Twain, Mark: pen name of Samuel Langhorne Clemens (1835–1910), American author and humorist, known particularly for his stories of the West and the Mississippi River, often reflecting the humorous tall tales of the time period, tales filled with hilarious exaggeration. Page 51.

20th Marines: a reserve unit of the Marine Corps. Page 16.

$20.67 an ounce: the price of an ounce of gold circa 1935. Page 15.

.22 bullet: a projectile having a diameter of .22 inches (.56 centimeters). Page 25.

tweren't: a short form for *it were not.* Page 166.

twig-bug: also *stick insect* or *walking stick,* an insect that looks like a twig. Most have long legs and a slender, wingless body that is 2 to 3 inches (5 to 8 centimeters) long. Page 95.

two-barb wire fence: a fence made of a type of strong wire that has barbs fastened on it. A *barb* is a short piece of wire twisted around the main wire and having sharp points that stick out. On *two-barb wire,* each barb has two sharp points. Some types of barbed wire have barbs with four sharp points. Barbed wire is used to prevent people or animals from entering or leaving a place, especially a field. Page 96.

2 x 2: a reference to a piece of wood measuring two inches (about 5 centimeters) on each side. *X* indicates dimensions, as in two inches by two inches. Page 134.

two-fisted: of stories or writing, describing events in a way that is tough and aggressive. Page 8.

type: classify as a member of a certain group that is seen as having particular behaviors or doing particular actions, etc. Page 108.

tyro: a beginner in learning anything; novice. Page 55.

U

unalloyed: not mixed with anything else, especially anything that would dilute it or any other feeling that would diminish it; pure; unqualified. Page 34.

Uncle Sam: the representation of the government of the United States, often pictured as a tall, thin man with white whiskers, wearing a blue coat, red-and-white-striped trousers and a top hat with a band of stars. (Used here humorously in reference to the governmental function of censorship.) Page 27.

Under the Black Ensign: an LRH pirate adventure set in the Caribbean during the seventeenth century. (An *ensign* is a flag flown by a ship and the *black ensign,* also called *black flag,* was traditionally flown by pirates.) Page 55.

Under the Die-Hard Brand: an LRH story first published in *Western Aces* magazine in March 1938. The son of a sheriff, disguised in his father's clothes, eliminates the town menace in a gunfight and restores the old sheriff's reputation. Page 69.

Unknown: a pulp magazine specializing in fantasy that was published by Street & Smith during the late 1930s and early 1940s. Page 40.

untrammeled: not limited or hindered. Page 120.

up in the air: not yet settled or decided; in suspense. Page 21.

up on (something), (be): know a lot about something. Page 32.

usher: escort (others) to their seats in a place such as a theater, restaurant, etc. Page 61.

U.S.M.C.: an abbreviation for the *United States Marine Corps*. Page 16.

V

"vacant shrine": part of a poem by John G. Neihardt (1881–1973), entitled "Let Me Live Out My Years," that was incorporated into the autobiographical novel *Martin Eden* (1909) by American novelist and short-story writer Jack London (1876–1916). The quoted lines are:

> *"Let me live out my years in heat of blood!*
> *Let me die drunken with the dreamer's wine!*
> *Let me not see this soul-house built of mud*
> *Go toppling to the dust—a vacant shrine!"* Page 108.

Vanguard to Steel: the working name of an LRH story first published as *All Frontiers Are Jealous* in *Five-Novels Monthly* magazine in June 1937. An American engineer surveying the route of a railway in Africa saves a girl from a fierce native tribe, then takes on the tribal chief in a face-to-face encounter. Page 20.

veddy: a spelling that represents an informal or humorous pronunciation of *very*. Page 130.

vein: 1. a particular manner or style of expressing something. Page 12.
2. a layer of a mineral in rock, especially an ore or a metal. Page 15.

vicarious: experienced through another person rather than firsthand. Page 77.

voodoo drums: drums, played in groups of three varying sizes, used in voodoo ceremonies. *Voodoo* is a body of beliefs and practices originally from Africa that includes magic and the supposed exercise of supernatural powers through the aid of spirits. Page 136.

W

wal: a spelling that represents a humorous pronunciation of *well,* used in introducing a statement. Page 112.

Waldorf-Astoria: originally the Waldorf, a luxury hotel constructed in the late 1800s in New York City, New York. Built by American millionaire William Waldorf Astor (1848–1919), it adjoined another luxury hotel, the Astoria, owned by his cousin. These hotels were operated as one and were known as the Waldorf-Astoria, with their 1,300 luxuriously furnished rooms making them the largest hotel complex in New York City during the 1890s. Both hotels were demolished in 1929 and, in 1931, a new Waldorf-Astoria hotel was built, occupying an entire city block. Page 71.

War Birds: a pulp magazine featuring aviation stories, published by Dell Publishing Company. Page 55.

war-whoop: a cry or yell as used in the past by Native North American warriors and other peoples when making an attack or rushing into battle. Page 33.

watercolor: an art or technique of painting using pigments (substances used to give paints their color) mixed with water rather than oil. Page 91.

way of, by: by means of; by the route of. Page 20.

weight around, chuck (one's): exercise (one's) power or influence, often to an excessive degree; give (one's) opinions (too) freely. In this context, *chuck* means throw and is used somewhat playfully to suggest the throwing of heavy things with ease or contempt; *weight* means influence, power or authority. Page 114.

Weird Tales: a pulp magazine first published in 1923, featuring stories of fantasy and horror fiction. Page 55.

welkin ring, made the: made a very loud noise. *Welkin* is an older word, now chiefly literary, meaning the sky, the vault of Heaven. Page 136.

Wells, H. G.: Herbert George Wells (1866–1946), English novelist and historian, best known for his science-fantasy novels with their predictions of future technology. Page 55.

Wellsville: a town about 40 miles (64 kilometers) southwest of Kansas City, Kansas, a state in the western part of the central United States. Page 112.

welt, raise a: cause a ridge or bump to appear on the skin by striking with a whip. Page 78.

West Indies: a large group of islands between North America and South America in the North Atlantic. Page 13.

whale of a: big, great or fine of its kind. Page 18.

whaler: a ship used in *whaling,* the work or industry of hunting and killing whales. Page 70.

wheel(s): a reference to the wheel used in *roulette,* a gambling game in which a ball is rolled onto a spinning horizontal wheel divided into compartments, with players betting on which compartment the ball will come to rest in. Page 15.

wherefore: for what purpose or reason; why. Page 31.

whipping your jinx: overcoming bad luck or misfortune. *Whip* means defeat or overcome, and a *jinx* is a person or thing believed to bring bad luck. Page 65.

white-knuckled: of stories or writing, causing fear or nervous excitement, with reference to the effect caused by gripping tightly to steady oneself. Page 8.

White Russian: the name given to members and supporters of the counterrevolutionary White armies, which fought against the Communist Red Army in the Russian Civil War (1918–1921). Page 107.

white slaving: an allusion to holding white people as slaves. Page 47.

whoa is me: *whoa* is used to mean stop or slow down. From the command to a horse when one wants him to stop. *Whoa is me* is used here as a humorous play on words for *woe is me,* an exclamation meaning I am distressed, unfortunate, in grief or the like. Page 98.

whole dog, go: a humorous variation of *go whole hog,* do something completely and thoroughly, go the whole way or to the fullest extent. Page 114.

wholesale scale, on a: in a large way, in large numbers or amount. Page 47.

wide: far away from or to one side of a point, mark, purpose or the like. Page 89.

Wilder: Thornton Wilder (1897–1975), American novelist and playwright. Page 109.

Wilson, Richard: (1920–1987) award-winning American science fiction writer. Wilson was instrumental in collecting and preserving many of the works and personal papers of early science fiction authors, which became part of the library collections at Syracuse University in New York. Page 145.

wit: the apt, clever and often humorous association of words or ideas or a capacity for it. Page 95.

wit, to: used to introduce a list or explanation of what one has just mentioned. Originally a phrase used in law, *that is to wit,* which meant that is to know, that is to say. Page 145.

Wodehouse: Sir Pelham Grenville Wodehouse (1881–1975), Anglo-American writer, born in England. His reputation as a humorous novelist was established in the early 1900s and he maintained popularity, with nearly one hundred novels depicting amusing characters in absurd and intricate situations. One of the best known films from his work in Hollywood during the 1930s was his adaptation of *Damsel in Distress,* his earlier novel, which became a film musical starring Fred Astaire. Page 78.

woodcraft: skill in traveling, living or working in the woods or forests. Page 32.

woodcut: a method of printing in which a block of wood carved with a picture or design is pressed into a coloring substance and then pressed onto paper or other surface to make a print. Page 91.

wood-pulp paper: a rough type of paper used for printing inexpensive magazines, etc. The low-cost pulp used in its manufacture is made from wood fibers. Page 55.

Woods, Clee: (1893–1990) a writer of western stories for both the pulps and Universal Pictures in the 1920s–1940s. Page 68.

woof and warp: the basic material or foundation of something (a structure, an entity, etc.). The phrase is a reference to the threads that make up a woven fabric: the *warp* threads run lengthwise on the loom and the *woof* threads run crosswise. A *loom* is a frame or machine on which thread is woven into cloth. Page 95.

wordage: the quantity or amount of words written, as over a period of time or for a given text, etc. Page 71.

word-weary: very tired of dealing with words, especially after one has been working with them, as in writing, for a long time. Page 2.

working title: a provisional title given to a book, film or other work before the final title is settled. Page 20.

World War ace: a fighter pilot during World War I (1914–1918), credited with destroying a prescribed number or more of enemy aircraft, usually five, in combat. Page 56.

Wormser, Dick: Richard Wormser (1908–1977), American author. His short stories appeared in pulp fiction magazines and, from the mid-1930s on, his film scripts were produced by Hollywood studios. His varied writing career also included award-winning works for younger audiences. Page 26.

worth, for what it's: a phrase used when offering a suggestion or opinion without making a claim as to its validity or value. Page 71.

wranglin': a shortening of *wrangling,* rounding up or tending horses or other livestock. Page 68.

wrastling: an informal variation of *wrestling.* Page 98.

wry: grimly humorous with a hint of bitterness. Page 2.

Y

Yafri: a legendary city built of massive blocks of stone, thought to have existed in the *Rub' al-Khali* (Arabic for Empty Quarter), the vast desert region of the southern Arabian Peninsula. Page 45.

yam: a spelling that represents a humorous pronunciation of *I am.* Page 113.

yarn: an entertaining story of real or fictitious adventures. Page 9.

Yellow Hair: the main character of L. Ron Hubbard's novel *Buckskin Brigades. Yellow Hair* is the Indian name of Michael Kirk, a blond white man raised as a scout and warrior by the Blackfeet. Page 34.

yore: a spelling that represents an informal pronunciation of *your.* Page 114.

"Young Charlotte": a nineteenth-century American ballad about a young girl whose male admirer takes her to a nearby village ball in an open sleigh on a freezing winter night. Wanting to be admired along the way, Charlotte refuses to wear proper clothes or a blanket, despite the bitter cold, and so arrives to the ball frozen to death. Page 90.

yowsah: a slang phrase meaning Yes, sir! that was first used in the 1930s by American bandleader and radio personality Ben Bernie (1891–1943). His radio programs, with his band The Lads, were among the most popular of the period. He would end the program with saying good night and "Yowsah, yowsah, yowsah, this is Ben Bernie and all The Lads." Page 96.

Z

Ziff-Davis: an American publishing company founded in 1927 in Chicago, Illinois, a state in the north central part of the United States. Page 137.

Zola: Émile Zola (1840–1902), French novelist whose works established a naturalistic style for French literature. In one of his most notable works, a series of twenty novels concerning five generations of one family, the author convincingly presents the people and society of the times. Page 129.

INDEX

voodoo drums

LRH playing, 136

W

Waldorf-Astoria, 71

Walsh, Gordon

letter to LRH in appreciation, 73

War Birds, 55

Wells, H. G.

Things to Come, 55

Western Romances

photograph of cover, 102

Tinhorn's Daughter, 103

westerns

writing, 68

Western Story, 28, 81, 112, 147

editor, John Burr, 82

featuring LRH tales, 80

West Indies

LRH in, 13

Where Angels Fear, 41

Wilder, 109

Wild West Weekly, 134

shorts for, 138

Wilson, Richard, 144

Woods, Clee

American Fiction Guild, 68

World Science Fiction Convention

photograph, 144

Wormser, Dick, 26

writers

action, goal of, 129

American Fiction Guild and, 86

average, description, 82

decent pulpateers and, 54

detective, 85

editors changing text of, 120

good or bad stories and, 36

Hollywood and, 26

LRH helping, 61

necessity to eat and, 63

pulp, description, 56

success and, 83

Would you tell me how to

write?, 61–91

"Writer's Cabin", 29

writing

adventure stories, 171

a letter of thanks to LRH, 73

anytime, anyplace and anything, 66

business of, 7–39

eating and, 71

good story, 68

paying bills and, 63

practice and, 65

WW II and, 145

Y

yarns

vigorous, convincing,

well-plotted, 25

writing and thinking up, 124

see also **stories**

Z

Zola, 129

THE
L. RON HUBBARD
SERIES

"To really know life," L. Ron Hubbard wrote, "you've got to be part of life. You must get down and look, you must get into the nooks and crannies of existence. You have to rub elbows with all kinds and types of men before you can finally establish what he is."

Through his long and extraordinary journey to the founding of Dianetics and Scientology, Ron did just that. From his adventurous youth in a rough and tumble American West to his far-flung trek across a still mysterious Asia; from his two-decade search for the very essence of life to the triumph of Dianetics and Scientology—such are the stories recounted in the L. Ron Hubbard Biographical Publications.

Drawn from his own archival collection, this is Ron's life as he himself saw it. With each volume of the series focusing upon a separate field of endeavor, here are the compelling facts, figures, anecdotes and photographs from a life like no other.

Indeed, here is the life of a man who lived at least twenty lives in the space of one.

FOR FURTHER INFORMATION VISIT
www.lronhubbard.org

The L. Ron Hubbard Series
A PROFILE

To order copies of *The L. Ron Hubbard Series*
or L. Ron Hubbard's Dianetics and
Scientology books and lectures, contact:

US AND INTERNATIONAL

BRIDGE PUBLICATIONS, INC.
5600 E. Olympic Blvd.
Commerce, California 90022 USA
www.bridgepub.com
Tel: (323) 888-6200
Toll-free: 1-800-722-1733

UNITED KINGDOM AND EUROPE

NEW ERA PUBLICATIONS
INTERNATIONAL ApS
Smedeland 20
2600 Glostrup, Denmark
www.newerapublications.com
Tel: (45) 33 73 66 66
Toll-free: 00-800-808-8-8008